Blue Willow

Revised Second Edition

Mary Frank Gaston

Collector Books
P.O. Box 3009
Paducah, Kentucky 42001

Searching For A Publisher?

We are always looking for knowledgeable people considered to be experts within their fields. If you feel that there is a real need for a book on your collectible subject and have a large comprehensive collection contact Collector Books.

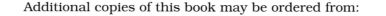

Additional copies of this book may be ordered from:

COLLECTOR BOOKS
P.O. Box 3009
Paducah, Kentucky 42002-3009

or

Mary Frank Gaston
P.O. Box 342
Bryan, Texas 77806

@ $14.95 each. Add $2.00 for postage and handling.

Copyright: Mary Frank Gaston, 1990.
Values updated 1996.

This book or any part thereof may not be reproduced without the written consent of the Author and Publisher.

Printed by IMAGE GRAPHICS, INC., Paducah, Kentucky

Other Books by Mary Frank Gaston

The Collector's Encyclopedia of Limoges Porcelain
The Collector's Encyclopedia of R.S. Prussia
The Collector's Encyclopedia of Flow Blue China
Haviland Collectables and Objects of Art
American Belleek
Antique Brass
Antique Copper
A Collector's Guide to Art Deco

These titles may be ordered from the author or the publisher. Include $2.00 each for postage and handling.

Mary Frank Gaston
P.O. Box 342
Bryan, Texas 77806

Collector Books
P.O. Box 3009
Paducah, KY 42001

To Jerry and Jeremy

Acknowledgments

As with most books, the final product is rarely accomplished without assistance from others. This one is no exception, and I would like to thank the many individuals who contributed to both the first edition of Blue Willow and this new revised survey. For the first book, I was indeed fortunate to have the help of Lois Misiewicz of Fallbrook, California. She was, in fact, the cornerstone for the book. She graciously invited me to her home to photograph her extensive collection and share her knowledge of the subject. She also suggested names of other collectors who could help, and she provided invaluable information and insights through *The Willow Notebook* which she published at that time.

From Lois and articles in *The Willow Notebook*, I learned about Connie Rogers who lived in Dayton, Ohio. She, too, kindly invited me to visit her to photograph her collection of fine pieces and examples of many different marks found on willow. Her publications in *The Willow Notebook, National Journal,* and *Depression Glass Daze* were extremely helpful. I also thank Conrad Biernacki of Toronto, Canada for his articles relating to Blue Willow in *The Willow Notebook* and the *National Journal* and for corresponding with me before the book was published. I am especially indebted to Connie and Conrad's work on Willow pattern identification which I used in the first edition and continue in this revised version of the book.

John Macy of Houston, Texas, gave me the idea of the "alphabet" approach to organizing the book. He had such a varied collection of objects with the Willow pattern that it seemed that type of layout would be both attractive and useful. Items featured on the cover of the first edition were also from John's collection.

Others who contributed to the first book were Glenwood and Martha Vernon, Brenham, Texas, who provided a large collection of Booths' pattern. I also thank Gladys M. Donham, Houston, Texas; Dunn & Ross Antiques, Houston, Texas; Grandfather's Trunk, Deland, Florida; Jesse and Harry Hall, Springboro, Ohio; Charlene and Don Johnson, Golden Age Antiques, Pawnee, Oklahoma; Nickerson's Antiques, Eldon, Missouri; Martha Schow, Trading Fair II, Houston, Texas; Carl Schluter and John Savell, S and S Outpost, Wallis, Texas; and Bettye Whitmire, Pastyme Antiques, Irving, Texas, for permitting me to photograph their Blue Willow for the first book.

My husband, Jerry, photographed all of the pieces for the first edition as well as drove us across the United States to visit collectors. For this revised work, most of the photographs were sent to me by collectors. We were fortunate, also, that two extensive collections were located only several hours from where we live in Texas.

Marcie Williams of Dallas invited us to photograph her Willow. Marcie has a very large assortment of different items with the Traditional pattern. Her collection reinforced the "ABC" approach to the book. Marcie is also interested in researching marks and provided some examples which were not shown in the first edition. Pieces featured on the cover are from Marcie's collection.

Rachel and Jim Lafferty, Commerce, Texas, also invited us to photograph Blue Willow which they have been collecting for over 40 years. After the first book was published, I was delighted to hear from Rachel, whom I had known when I worked in the Registrar's Office at East Texas State University. Jim had also been one of my professors. I admit I was not "into" Willow at the time (some 25 or so years ago), and thus did not know of their "addiction." It was a pleasure to visit with them again. I just wish now I had then their foresight to amass such a wonderful collection of lovely and unusual pieces.

I thank the many collectors who sent photographs. I was able to include many items which would not have been possible otherwise. The collectors photographed each piece and provided information on size, marks, and pattern. I sincerely appreciate the efforts of a long list of individuals.

Lynda P. Lehmann-Galloway, now residing in Austin (formerly of Florida), sent numerous photographs of pieces and marks. She has concentrated on collecting the Burleigh pattern and examples of Willow with different manufacturer's marks. In her search, she has unearthed some rare marks which have been documented by British authority, Geoffrey A. Godden, in personal correspondence with Lynda. She graciously shared her information with me concerning her examples and marks.

Scott D. Johnson, Marketing and Sales Coordinator for Heritage Mint, Ltd, provided photographs and information on the Blue Willow products his firm produces and distributes.

I also thank the following:

Captain J. Gordon Bengtson, Westboro, MA
Alan and Shirley Bradley, Saskatoon, Canada
Samuel Ravenel Gaillard, Summerville, SC
Elva Hughes, Hinsdale, MA
Hubert and Dessa King, Hurst, TX
Mary L. Smith, Tallahassee, FL
Peter and Susan Steelman
Jamie Stott, Vancouver, WA
Angelina Tagliaferri, Mansfield, TX

I thank the following members of the Ohio Willow Club:

Beth Atherton, Chagrin Falls
Betty Blakeslee, Cleveland Heights
Nancee Blaney, Ashland
Arlene Corrigan, Cleveland
Michael L. Curtner, Sidney
Lucille Egger, Columbus
W. Lowell Fenner, Cincinnati
Harry J. Hall, Springboro
C. Stephen Hunter, Cincinnati
Marjory La Londe, Avon
Betty Ann Smiddy, Cincinnati
Mary Shafer Smith, Cincinnati

Last, but by no means least, I thank Connie Rogers who helped tremendously in this revised work. Needless to say, her lovely collection has increased since I visited her in 1982! Her son, Scot, made excellent photographs of her vast collection and those owned by members of the Ohio Club. Thank you, Scot for such fine work. Connie provided a very large number of pictures which entailed a lot of work in listing all of the necessary information. She also sent me copies of articles about Willow she has written during the last several years (see the Bibliography). Connie now publishes the *American Willow Report*, a bi-monthly publication, which furnishes an abundance of news about Willow to collectors. Most of all I thank Connie for the time she spent reading the final manuscript of this edition, making corrections, and offering suggestions. Her help was invaluable.

Preface

Although the Blue Willow pattern on ceramics has been criticized since its invention, criticism has not deterred the loyal devotees of this most popular of all patterns. The design has managed to hold its own quite well for nearly 200 years. The popularity of the pattern has not faded with time or life style changes as fads and fashions usually do. Today, companies in many countries including America, England, and Japan manufacture all types of ceramic articles decorated with the Blue (or often some other color) Willow pattern. Additionally, one can find a myriad of other contemporary objects ranging from plastics to linens with this distinctive blue and white design.

People have collected Blue Willow throughout its history, but the pattern's collectability is probably at its height today. The number of collectors is constantly increasing—and in an organized manner too. "Willow" clubs for "Willowers" are found in towns throughout the United States and also in Canada.

This book is designed to show a wide range of antique and collectable Blue Willow. An adequate supply of such items is still available for collectors. Because of the number and diversity of articles exhibiting this pattern, the photographs are laid out in ABC fashion by type of item. Some contemporary items and a few non-ceramic items are included to demonstrate the unending passion for the Blue Willow pattern. Today's items will surely find their niche in antique history during the next 200 years!

A section of manufacturer's marks precedes the color photographs of objects. The marks are arranged differently in this revised edition, grouped by English, Japanese, and American companies. A glossary of terms pertinent to ceramics that might prove beneficial to collectors is included at the end of the book. An Object index with a cross reference to items commonly known by more than one name has been added. A broader grouping of objects has been made. For example, the photographic section on "CUPS" includes all kinds of cups such as Punch Cup, Measuring Cup, Mustache Cup, and so forth, instead of each of these appearing under the section "P" or "M". Consult the Object index if a particular item is not pictured in the section where you first look for it.

Two indexes of Manufacturers have been included for English and American willow. An index for willow of Japanese origin has also been compiled. Another index including the few photographs of willow made in countries other than England, the United States, and Japan follows the index of American manufacturers. An index of Patterns (with the exception of the Traditional pattern) follows the Object index.

The Price Guide is located at the end of the book. Prices are keyed to the photograph numbers. A price range is quoted for items illustrated in the book. Please keep in mind that prices are influenced by a multitude of factors including condition, availability, and demand. Ultimately the collector must be the judge of the value of a particular piece. The prices shown in this book are intended to be used only as a guide. Price information was obtained from dealers, collectors, sales, and shops throughout the United States in order to give as accurate a reflection as possible of current Blue Willow prices. Figures stated assume that items are in good-to-mint condition.

I hope you enjoy browsing through the Blue Willow Alphabet. I am still searching, however, for that "Z" item!

Mary Frank Gaston
P.O. Box 342
Bryan, TX 77806

Please include a SASE when writing. I regret that I will be unable to reply to written comments or questions if a SASE is not included.

Contents

The Blue Willow Legend

The story on the back of this book is but one of many legends connected with the ceramic items displaying the popular Blue Willow pattern. The stories vary in length and content—some are short, some are long, some are simple, and some are quite elaborate. Because there are so many, I cannot reproduce them all here.

The elements that make up the overall design of the Willow pattern, however, all have a special significance in each legend, but the essence of each is usually quite similar: A wealthy Chinese father (usually referred to as the Mandarin) wishes his daughter (Hong Shee, Koong-shee, or Li-chi are some of the names for her) to marry a man he has chosen (his accountant or secretary, or a duke or an older person of wealth and prestige). The daughter, however, is in love with a young man (usually called Chang). The young lovers decide to run away before the prearranged marriage takes place. They are not completely successful, for depending on the particular legend, the couple is eventually pursued

either by the father or the bridegroom-to-be, or Chang is killed by the bridegroom, or both Chang and the daughter die. The couple is not destined to be parted, though, for ultimately in most legends the gods change the two into a pair of turtle doves so that they may be together forever.

People enjoy collecting these various stories as well as the dishes with the Blue Willow pattern they describe. When comparing the story to the design on a plate, the pattern does seem to come to life. You find yourself actually believing the legend through its illustration.

But turning from legend to fact, it is interesting to note that the Blue Willow legends were not created until after the Blue Willow pattern on china became popular. Also the legends are not Chinese in origin as is sometimes thought. The stories were invented by the English and Americans. And the pattern, as we know it, was designed by the English and not the Chinese.

History of the Blue Willow Pattern

Although the Blue Willow pattern was not originally designed by the Chinese, its inspiration, of course, definitely was influenced by the Chinese. The major components of the pattern, namely the willow tree, the orange tree, and tea house all relate to Oriental culture. These elements had been used by the Chinese for centuries to decorate their porcelain wares. The English as well as other West Europeans greatly admired the beautiful porcelain which had been imported from China since the 1600's. Those items were decorated with hand-painted blue underglaze Oriental themes. Attempts were made again and again in Europe to reproduce those items, both in body and decoration. Efforts were not successful, though, until the mid-1700's.

The successful evolution of the Blue Willow pattern was due to two factors: one, the transfer method of decoration; and two, the technique of underglaze decoration. (Please see the Glossary for a description of these terms.) Although pottery as

an industry was started in the Staffordshire district of England in the mid-1600's, the products were earthenware and not translucent porcelain like the Chinese wares. The English ceramics of this period were decorated by hand and over the glaze. Transfer printed designs and underglaze decoration were not in use in England until after 1760.

The transfer method of decoration allowed the same design or pattern to be used over and over again. It could be applied either over or under the glaze and used on any type of ceramic body. This method of decoration was much less expensive than hand painting. Decoration could be more elaborate, and many and all kinds of objects could be decorated with the same pattern. The technique of transfer designs over the glaze was practiced in England during the 1750's.

It was not until the 1760's, however, that the method of transfer printing under the glaze was perfected. Underglaze printing was preferred to overglaze printing because it made the pattern permanent. Decoration over the glaze could be marred or worn off. The Chinese had known the technique of underglaze decoration for hundreds of years, and the products imported from China had handpainted underglaze decoration. The Chinese had discovered that the color blue, derived from cobalt, was the one color which could withstand the high degrees of heat necessary to fire the glaze and still maintain the clarity of the design. That is why the oriental porcelains were decorated with blue and white designs. That is also why the Blue Willow pattern originated in blue rather than in some other color. So the English, wanting to copy the Chinese style, designs, and colors, discovered it was necessary to use the color blue if they wanted underglaze decoration.

Thomas Turner of the Caughley Pottery in Staffordshire is usually credited with being the first (circa 1780) to engrave a Willow pattern, and transfer it underglaze. Thomas Minton, an apprenticed engraver for the Caughley factory and later a master engraver in London, also designed Willow patterns at about that time. But the Spode factory, not Turner or Minton, is attributed as the inventor (circa 1790) of the pattern that ultimately became the traditional Blue Willow pattern.

According to Robert Copeland, in his book *Spode's Willow Pattern and Other Designs after the Chinese,* the traditional Blue Willow pattern is actually Spode's Willow III which was designed circa 1810. Spode's original Willow I and II (designed around 1790) differ from the Traditional pattern (Willow III) chiefly in the border designs and method of engraving the transfer pattern.

Copeland also notes, as do others, that the term "Willow" was used for ceramics decorated with Oriental themes prior to the Spode designs. But there is no consensus about when the term originated or why the earliest English Oriental patterns and later Spode's patterns were called "Willow" in the first place. The patterns could have been called by other names of other designs featured in the pattern.

My guess is that the term "Willow" evolved as a pattern name because the tree form used by the Chinese for decoration on their porcelain was the most recognizable to the English of any of the decoration themes on Oriental wares. Thus, they called the tree form "Willow," eventually using the term to describe patterns containing such a tree form design.

Once the methods of transfer printing and underglaze decoration were perfected, the English potters were in a good position to compete with the Oriental imported ceramic goods. They could manufacture all of the blue and white dishes that the English desired, and most importantly at a price they could afford. An enormous market was available for the products, not only in England but in America and Canada as well.

During the 1800's most English potteries produced a version of the Blue Willow pattern. The pattern was applied to all classes of ceramics beginning with semi-porcelain in the early days and later extending to stoneware, ironstone, and bone china. These terms concerning the body types of ceramics are defined in the Glossary. Knowledge of the different body types is important for collectors. The body type may determine the condition of a particular piece and in turn its desirability and its price. By becoming familiar with the characteristics of the various classes of ceramics, one is often able to distinguish the old from the new, and to determine the country of origin if the example is not marked.

England was the first country to manufacture Blue Willow. However, many other countries also followed suit. Japan is probably the next largest producer of the pattern. Many examples from that country were imported to the United States from the late 1880's to the present. Potteries in the United States also manufactured a large amount of the pattern during the 20th century, especially during the 1920's and 1930's. Examples are also seen from Belgium, France, Germany, Holland, Ireland, Mexico, Poland, Portugal, and Spain. And although the Chinese did not design the Blue Willow pattern originally, Oriental potters did use the pattern for decorating ceramics after it became so popular in England!

Blue Willow Patterns

The traditional Blue Willow pattern is considered to be the one designed by Spode. However, when people say they collect Blue Willow, that does not usually mean that they collect only pieces with the Traditional (Spode type) pattern. Numerous other versions of the Willow pattern have been manufactured through the years by other companies in England as well as companies in other countries. There are probably about as many, if not more, versions of the Blue Willow pattern as there are versions of the legend connected with the pattern. There is not just *one* Blue Willow legend, likewise there is not just *one* Blue Willow pattern.

Some years ago, I personally learned that all Blue Willow patterns are not the same. I had just opened an antique business specializing in all types of dinner services. One day a lady brought in a Blue Willow plate. She needed one more to complete a dinner service for eight. I told her I would try to find such a plate for her, and carefully made a note of the manufacturer's mark. While on a buying trip, I did indeed find a Blue Willow plate. Returning home, I immediately called the lady who promptly came (from some distance, too) to pick up her plate. However, my plate did not *exactly* match hers even though it had the same mark. Needless to say, she was very disappointed. I learned that in the future I must really look closely at the details of the Blue Willow pattern I was trying to match and not just the maker's mark - for often the same maker made more than one version of that pattern!

The traditional Blue Willow pattern contains many components. (See Plate 339 for one example). The outer border is composed of several scroll and geometric designs. An inner border of geometric designs frames the center pattern. This center pattern features a tea house with a pavilion on the right side. An orange tree (often called an apple tree) is behind the tea house. A willow tree is almost centered in the design. In front of the willow tree is a bridge with three people. A boat with a person in it is to the top left of the willow tree, and above the boat is another Oriental style building and a fir tree. A zig-zag fence is at the bottom of the design, and two birds facing each other are at the top of the pattern.

Many manufacturers used transfers with the exact version of this Spode pattern or altered it only slightly. But other companies had their own interpretation of the pattern. Also, as I noted, some potteries manufactured more than one version of the pattern. We find that some Blue Willow patterns have no birds while others have flocks. Also the shape, size, and direction of flight of the birds may vary. The number of the people in the pattern many range from none to five. The shape of the bridge may differ as well as the position of the buildings, willow tree, and boat, and there may be more than one boat in the pattern. Some patterns are reversed by having usual right-handed components of the pattern on the left and vice versa. Sometimes only a part of the willow design is used to decorate items. The blue color may range from very dark to quite light, or the pattern may not be blue at all, but some other color or group of colors.

Because of such variations, it appears at first glance that it would be impossible to find any points of similarity for the different willow patterns manufactured by so many different companies throughout the years. But that is not really so. Many of the willow pattern variations do have some basic features in common that are related to border and center design.

Conrad Biernacki and Connie Rogers, both advanced Willow collectors, have done extensive work in categorizing these different borders and center patterns. Although they note that the categories are not all-inclusive for every willow pattern ever made, I find that the categories are quite helpful not only for collectors who are trying to match pieces, but also for beginning collectors to acquaint them with the different willow patterns. I also think that being able to categorize many of the willow patterns adds another interesting dimension to this field of collecting.

I use these categories to describe many of the examples in this book. Please note that the majority of pieces featured have the Traditional pattern, either in whole or in part. Thus, I do not state that information in the caption of most pieces or list by photograph number examples of the Traditional pattern in the Pattern Index at the end of the book. The pattern is assumed to be Traditional or a component of the Traditional pattern if no pattern information is included with the caption.

The following terms and numbers for categories of Willow Pattern Borders and Center Patterns are those used in articles by Conrad Biernacki in the *National Journal* and by Conrad Biernacki and Connie Rogers in *The Willow Notebook* which are listed in the bibliography. I have included brief descriptions of these categories and indicated one photograph example of each, but please see these articles and Robert Copeland's *Spode's Willow Pattern and Other Designs After the Chinese* for more detailed descriptions and historical information.

——— Willow Border Patterns ———

1. **Traditional.** This border is the Spode border design for Willow III. A wheel or circular design is the main characteristic of this pattern. See Photograph 339.
2. **Butterfly or Insect or Fitzhugh.** This border is named for the winged antennaed designs in the pattern, or called "Fitzhugh" for a person by that name who supposedly commissioned a set of china to be made with this particular style of border. See Photograph 125.
3. **Bow Knot.** Four-section loop shapes characterize this border. See Photograph 305.
4. **Dagger or Fleur-De-Lis.** Tiny pointed designs are on the inside of the border pointed toward the center pattern. See Photograph 337.
5. **Scroll and Flower.** Fancy curved designs are combined with floral patterns. See Photographs 319 and 350.
6. **Floral.** This type of border is composed chiefly of floral designs. See Photograph 352. Floral borders #1 and #2 (see Photographs 352 and 379) are the two most often found on simple rubber stamp patterns made by American companies.
7. **Pictorial.** Miniature or cameo willow pattern designs compose the outer border. See Photograph 353.
8. **Simple Line.** Only one or two solid colored ring type or a series of short lines form the border. See Photographs 6 and 311.
9. **Borderless.** These patterns have no outer border. See Photograph 335.

Mr. Biernacki notes that there are variations in the border patterns, especially in the Scroll and Flower, Floral, and Pictorial categories. He suggests that one should also indicate the name of the manufacturer, if known, and any pattern name that might be included in the mark when describing items with these types of borders that differ from the one most commonly seen.

——— Willow Center Patterns ———

1. **Traditional.** This is the center pattern referred to earlier that is based on the original Spode design for their Willow III. This is the most common willow center pattern. The pattern is characterized by 4 figures (3 on a 3 arch bridge, 1 in a boat), 2 birds, a tea house, the willow and orange trees, and a fence in the foreground. There is also an inner border of geometric designs. Mr. Biernacki notes that the Japanese versions of the Traditional pattern do not usually have this inner border. See Photographs 339 (English) and 368 (Japanese). The Traditional pattern usually has the Traditional border pattern.
2. **Booths.** This center pattern is named for the pattern used by the Booth company in England. The pattern is similar to the Traditional pattern except there is no fence in the foreground. The willow tree has six branches on the left and 3 on the right. The Bow Knot border pattern is used with this center design. Two Phoenix or Double Phoenix are two of the marks found on Japanese copies of this particular pattern. Other English factories such as Wood & Sons also used a similar center pattern, but they called it by a different name. See Photograph 305.
3a. **Two Temples I.** This pattern name and the following (Two Temples II) were given by Spode to one of the most popular Chinese landscape designs which were copied by English potters. Two Temples I is distinguished by two seemingly overlapping temples on the left side of the pattern, 4 figures (two on the one arch bridge, one in the temple doorway, one on the rocks), and no birds. The position of the willow tree is below the bridge. The placement of the willow tree, which differs in Two Temples I and Two Temples II, is the easiest way to differentiate between the two patterns. The design has a Butterfly border. See Photograph 347.

3b. **Two Temples II.** This pattern is similar to Two Temples I except there are only 3 figures (two on the one arch bridge, and one in the temple doorway) in the pattern. The willow tree is positioned Above the bridge in the pattern. The Butterfly border is not exactly the same as the one used for Two Temples I. This version of the Two Temples pattern is more common than Two Temples I. Sometimes the pattern is reversed. See Photographs 348 and 426 (reversed).

4. **Mandarin.** This willow center pattern has only 1 figure located on the boat, and there is no bridge. It has a Dagger border. This pattern was called Mandarin II in my first edition, but Mandarin is sufficient. Robert Copeland, in his book *Spode's Willow Pattern and Other Designs After the Chinese,* used the terms "Mandarin I or II" to indicate different types of ceramic body (earthenware or porcelain) with the pattern. See Photograph 337.

5. **Worcester.** This center pattern is named for the pattern used by the Worcester Royal Porcelain Company in England. It has 3 figures and 3 boats but no orange or willow tree. It has a Scroll and Flower border. See Plate 319.

6. **Burleigh.** This pattern is named for one design found on items manufactured by the English company of Burgess and Leigh. The pattern has 5 figures but no orange tree. It has a Scroll and Flower border. See Photograph 331.

7. **Turner.** This pattern is named for John Turner, an English potter who originated the design circa 1810-1812 (Coysh, pp. 14-15, 1971). The pattern has 2 figures and no birds. It has a Scroll and Flower border. The Turner pattern was most widely used by Masons' factory. See Photograph 350.

8. **Simplified.** This category is for the versions of the willow pattern that show only a part of the pattern. They may have a Floral, Pictorial, or Simple Line border, or no border at all. See photographs 351 and 352.

9. **Polychrome.** This term denotes any multi-colored variant pattern. See Photograph 355. Please note that in this edition, "Polychrome" is used to describe only Variant patterns. "Multi-colored" is the term used to describe all other versions of the willow pattern if the pattern contains more than one color. Polychrome and multi-colored are, of course, synonymous terms.

10. **Canton.** This category of pattern includes the early handpainted Chinese patterns and also the English and American copies of these patterns. See Photographs 332 and 333 for examples of English and American versions of the Canton pattern.

In using these Border and Center Pattern categories to describe the photographs, I use the Traditional term if the essential elements for that pattern are basically the same: the number and position of buildings, willow and orange tree, bridge, people, birds, and boat. As I noted, some of the renditions of the Traditional category appear to have some variations as to shape of trees, boat, people, birds, etc. They are not considered variants, however, unless for example, the pattern has four birds rather than two.

I use the term "Two Temples Variant" to describe examples of this pattern that may be Simplified but also have only two figures, or have birds which are not the characteristics of either Two Temples I or II. However, they still have "two temples" as the dominating characteristic. Likewise, I refer to the Simplified pattern of Two Temples II as Two Temples II Simplified rather than just Simplified to further identify the pattern. In most instances I do not use category 9 (Polychrome) alone if one of the center patterns is identifiable as one of the Center categories or a variant of one. I include that information also in the description.

Dating Blue Willow

A particular version of the Blue Willow pattern usually cannot be used as a guide for dating specific pieces. There has really been no time period, even in the early years, when just one Blue Willow pattern was manufactured. Also the various components that make up the pattern such as the number of oranges (or apples) on the tree, the shape of the bridge or buildings, the number of people, or presence or absence of birds, or the fence in the design cannot be used for dating the pattern. Copeland notes that the blue of the early patterns was quite dark, but through the years manufacturing processes became more sophisticated which allowed the pattern to be produced in all shades of blue. This holds true for today as well with the pattern being seen in various blue shades.

Many pieces of Blue Willow were not marked by the manufacturer, especially during the early period. Marks, however, are perhaps the most accurate method of finding out the time period for many of the examples available to the collector. If the piece is unmarked, the body of the object often gives a clue to the period of manufacture. Familiarity with the various body types and glazes can be accomplished by examining marked examples of the pattern from the early, middle, and late periods. Knowledge gained from such examination will provide good clues to help in determining whether an unmarked piece was made 10, 50 or 100 years ago.

Manufacturers' marks usually do not tell you the exact year a specific piece was made, but the time period a mark was in use can often be known. Most collectors like to know as much as possible about what they collect. Knowledge of the time a particular company used a certain mark and the beginning and closing dates of a company aid in this search.

The mark of the manufacturer is found on the back or base of an object in one of three forms: incised, impressed or printed (see the Glossary for a description of these terms). Incised, impressed, and underglaze printed marks are basically considered to be permanent, meaning that they cannot be worn off or taken off. Sometimes examples are seen where this has been attempted, either by grinding out the mark, or placing another mark over the original one. This is especially true for items of Japanese or German origin following World War II. English marks are found in all three forms appearing either singly or in combination. The majority are printed, however. American, Japanese, and most other countries' marks on Blue Willow are of the printed type.

Because of extensive and intensive research, namely by England's Geoffrey A. Godden, Blue Willow of English origin is perhaps easier to date than examples from other countries. Because such a large portion of Blue Willow was made in England, collectors should be aware of several points which can help in interpreting English marks.

A rope-like symbol shaped like a bow is sometimes seen printed on English ceramics. The mark may or may not contain initials which can identify the company of manufacture. This symbol is known as the Staffordshire Knot because it was used by many potteries in the Staffordshire district of England.

An impressed or printed diamond symbol with letters and numbers or just printed numbers prefaced with the initials "RD" are sometimes found on items either alone or combined with other types of marks. Such marks indicate that the pattern or mold (shape) of the object was registered with the English Patent Office in order to keep that particular pattern or mold from being copied by some other manufacturer. The diamond mark was instituted in 1843, and when decoded, the month, day, and year of registration can be determined. This system continued until 1883. In 1884, a consecutive numbering system starting with "RD1" replaced the former method. General books on marks usually give the tables for decoding the diamond symbol, and also show what numbers the patents had reached on the first of January of each year starting with 1885 through about 1900 for the consecutive numbering system. Thus, if an example has an "RD" number that falls between the numbers listed for January of 1885 and January 1886, the design was registered sometime during 1885.

These English registry marks are often misinterpreted. The dates refer to the time the design or shape was *first* registered - not when a particular piece was made. The piece had to be made after the design was registered so that the manufacturer would know what letters or numbers to put on the piece. But it is often stated that from the diamond shape one can date exactly pieces so marked, or from the registry number, the exact year the piece was made can be known. The first pieces of a particular registered design or shape may have been made during the year shown by the mark, but not on that day of the month decoded from the diamond shape registry mark. Most importantly, the same design or shape may have been used for several or many years, and the same registry mark would apply. Also not all pieces manufactured from 1842 on had a registry mark of either kind. The registry numbers and marks are useful only as a clue to the period when the pattern or shape was first invented.

It is generally accepted that the word "England" (or any other country's name) in a mark indicates a date later than 1890. The McKinley Tariff Act of 1890 stated that goods imported to this country must be marked with a country of origin. However, some manufacturers used England (or whatever country) in their marks before that time. Also some pieces manufactured after that time might not be marked at all - for example, all pieces in a set of China. "Made in England" is considered to be a 20th century mark. The words "Trade Mark" and "Ltd." in English marks were not in use until after 1862.

Many English potteries at certain periods in their history devised their own methods and codes for dating their products. Copeland, Minton, Wedgwood, and Worcester are some examples. Detailed information on decoding these marks can be obtained from general books on marks.

Perhaps the most common mistake in attributing English marked wares is when the mark includes the name "Wedgwood". Several companies used this name in their marks. All "Wedgwood" marks do not refer to Josiah Wedgwood, founder, circa 1759, of the famous Wedgwood company. His marks are impressed or printed. He did not spell his name with an "e" (Wedgewood), nor did he use the initial "J" in his marks, or use the mark of "Wedgwood & Co". Godden states that a John Wedge Wood operated a pottery from 1841 to 1860 and used a mark that incorporated the name J. Wedgwood. He notes that an impressed WEDGWOOD alone or WEDGWOOD & CO. is probably that of Ralph Wedgwood, circa 1780 to 1800. The impressed WEDGWOOD can thus be confusing for Josiah Wedgwood did use such a mark. But according to Godden, the ceramic body of pieces with this mark are not up to par with that of Josiah's company. Podmore, Walker, and Co., circa 1860, also used Wedgwood & Co. in their marks. The Wedgwood was for Enoch Wedgwood who was associated with the company. See Wedgwood & Co. marks a, b, and c.

For the English marks shown in this book, I have included dates where possible. These dates indicate the time the mark was first used by a company or the time period during which the company used the mark. These dates are based on information from Geoffrey A. Godden's *Encyclopedia of British Pottery and Porcelain,* 1964. See this book for more detailed historical information of the English potteries. A few of the English marks show Godden's name in parentheses with a date. This refers to entries under his name in the Bibliography which document the marks through personal correspondence between Mr. Godden and Lynda Galloway, one of the contributors of marks and information to this book.

Blue Willow of Japanese origin is largely from the 20th century. Ceramics are marked with different symbols and initials combined with or only marked "Japan," "Made in Japan," or "Made in Occupied Japan." It is not possible usually to say what particular company or potter the marks stand for. Sometimes we find that the marks are just for American importing companies. Thus it is difficult to date 20th century Japanese wares more precisely than certain time periods.

From 1891 to 1921, the word "Nippon" was used alone or with symbols to mark ceramic ware made in Japan for export. "Nippon" was the name the country was called during this period. Also "Made in Nippon" is sometimes seen. In 1921, "Nippon" was discontinued in marks to comply with United States customs laws which determined that the word "Nippon" would not suffice any longer to designate country of origin, and that the imported items must use "Japan" to designate the country. Thus, after September 1921 until c. 1940, and after 1953, "Made in Japan," or "Japan" was used to mark Japanese products. It is sometimes suggested that "Made in Japan" was only used from 1921 to 1940, and that "Japan" alone was only used after 1953. However, by comparing examples with these marks, it is evident that some items just marked "Japan" are older than some marked "Made in Japan," and some items marked "Made in Japan" appear to be later than 1940. After World War II, from c. 1948 to 1953, "Occupied Japan," or "Made in Occupied Japan," was included with Japanese marks or used alone to designate that Japan was occupied by a foreign country. Due to the short time period this type of mark was used, items so marked are often higher in price than other ware of Japanese origin. Paper labels were used from the Nippon era to the present to denote country of origin on Japanese goods. Because they are easily removable, many Japanese items must be relegated to the "unmarked" category.

We find that the first Blue Willow pattern produced in the United States was by the Buffalo Pottery Company of Buffalo, New York, in 1905. After that time, many other American potteries produced Blue Willow items. But it is important to remember that American examples of Blue Willow do not date prior to 1905 even though the particular pottery may have been in business many or several years before the Buffalo Pottery first perfected the underglaze Blue Willow pattern.

Since the first edition of my book was published, *Lehner's Encyclopedia of U.S. Marks on Pottery, Por-*

celain, & Clay by Lois Lehner, an authority on American marks, has been released by Collector Books (1988). This book is truly an invaluable reference for collectors of all types of American pottery, including Blue Willow. Numerous examples of marks for the various American companies who produced the Blue Willow pattern are shown. In many instances, these marks now can be dated in a more specific manner. General time periods when the marks shown here were used or the company's dates of operation (if mark dates are uncertain) are indicated in the American marks where possible based on information contained in Ms. Lehner's book. In some cases, dating codes were used by factories. Particular marks can be decoded by referring to the tables or information in Lehner's Encyclopedia for companies such as Buffalo, Homer Laughlin, and Walker, for example.

Collecting Blue Willow

Just as there is not just one Blue Willow legend or just one Blue Willow pattern, there is not just one category of Blue Willow collector. Some collect only the old while others collect not just for age but for type of item as well. Some concentrate on English or American examples. Some prefer one particular company's pattern while others are interested in acquiring examples of as many different maker's marks as possible.

Due to the pattern's long history, one finds examples dating from many different time periods. English pieces from the early 1800's (some of which are in museums) to 1880 are classified as true antiques as they are over 100 years old. Many examples from the latter part of this period are available for collectors. Numerous items manufactured in countries other than England, such as Japan and the United States during the latter part of the 19th century and early 20th century, are fast approaching this "antique" status. Additionally, pieces dating from the 1930's to 1950's are definitely considered collectable as well as more recent items from the 1960's and 1970's that are collected due to their uniqueness or scarcity. One can say that this field of collecting has something for everyone ranging from antique to modern and from inexpensive knick knacks to articles of museum quality.

Blue Willow items show not only a variation in type of object but also a variation in quality. The quality depends on the type of ceramic body and the particular manufacturer. Concerning ceramic body, hard paste porcelain and bone china are the most exquisite in appearance as they are translucent and light in weight, but also durable. Ironstone and stoneware are quite durable but are heavy in texture and appearance. Semi-porcelain is the least durable for it is fired at lower temperatures than porcelain and stoneware. Earthenwares break more easily, and they also are subject to crazing because they are not fired at high enough temperatures to fuse the body and the glaze. Glazes on earthenwares vary from thin and easily scratched to glossy and impenetrable. The majority of Blue Willow items are earthenwares. However, depending on the manufacturer and the time period when the pieces were manufactured, some earthenwares are of fine quality with first rate decoration and color while some porcelain examples may have poor decoration. Transfer designs range on all classes of ceramic bodies from beautifully clear and distinct to faint or smudged. Because of this variation in workmanship, collectors learn to be choosy and consider the quality of the overall piece as well as the particular item when adding to their collection.

Other important facets for collectors of Blue Willow are examples of the Willow pattern in colors other than blue or multi-colored patterns. During the first quarter of the 19th century, transfer designs in other colors were tried and eventually perfected. Black, brown, and mulberry were among the first that met with success. From the turn of this century to the present, we find that the Willow pattern has been made in practically every color.

The multi-colored or polychromed willow items are quite striking in appearance. In the early days, the different colors were applied by hand over the glaze to the underglaze Blue Willow pattern. The Buffalo Pottery in the United States was not only the first American company to produce a Blue Willow pattern underglaze, but it was also the first to have a multi-colored version. As technology increased, it was possible to make multi-colored patterns under the glaze as well. Some examples of the pattern in other colors and multi-colors are shown in the photographs.

Historically, Blue Willow items have been inexpensive. From the late 1800's to the present, Blue Willow items have been sold through catalog ordering companies, variety stores, and even given as premiums with certain products. Price-wise, today we find that the handpainted multi-colored pieces and early examples in other solid colors are the most expensive. For standard Blue Willow tableware items, those of English origin are more costly than similar Japanese and American ones. In most fields of collecting, the older the pieces, the higher the prices. However, as noted earlier, because willow collecting encompasses such a broad time period together with a stable popularity of the pattern that makes new items as equally acceptable by many collectors as the old, this rule of thumb does not always hold true. Many modern items may cost as much or more than the genuinely old ones. In fact,

in the past collectors have often been able to purchase really rare, old, and unusual items for quite small sums. But as collector interest increases and sellers become more knowledgeable, prices escalate for these kinds of pieces. This is quite apparent from current prices on Blue Willow items seen at shops and shows. In fact, it has only been within the last few years that very much Blue Willow has been seen at antique shows. If the quality of the piece is good, if it is old, or if it is unusual, the item should command a premium. Cake stands, cheese dishes, cruet sets, infant feeders, mustard pots, and wash sets are just a few of such items pictured here. Take a careful look at these Blue Willow treasures so that you won't pass up a real "find"!

Happy Blue Willowing!

Marks

The manufacturers' marks are divided into four sections in this edition. The first section contains English marks. In the descriptions of the photographs, the manufacturer's name is included (if known), and readers may refer to that name in the Marks to find the mark on that particular item. The English marks are arranged alphabetically by manufacturer. If more than one mark is shown for a factory, they are lettered "a," "b," "c," etc., and the information in the caption of the photograph will indicate which specific mark: for example, Doulton mark c. If the particular mark is not included in the Marks section, the information known about the mark is printed in the caption, or the reader is referred to a specific mark number (or a page) in Geoffrey A. Godden's *Encyclopedia of British Pottery and Porcelain Marks*. A few English marks have not been identified. These are shown at the end of the English Marks. They are called "Unidentified English Marks a, b, c," etc.

The second section illustrates a variety of Japanese marks. These are arranged by type of Japanese name rather than by factory. Nippon is first, followed by Made in Japan, Made in Occupied Japan, and Japan. Each group's marks are lettered "a," "b," "c," etc. The description of the photograph will indicate whether the mark is "Made in Japan" mark a, or "Made in Occupied Japan" mark d, for example. Most of the Japanese pieces, however, will just have "Japan," or "Japanese" in the description rather than a particular mark. Most of the Japa-

nese marks shown were on items which were not included in the photographs, such as plates, platters, etc. with the Traditional pattern. The number and variety of these marks, however, are of interest to collectors.

The third section includes a number of American marks. These are arranged alphabetically by manufacturer, and are labeled "a," "b," "c," etc., if more than one mark is shown for a company. Like the Japanese marks, not all of the American marks have a corresponding example in the photographs. If a mark of a photographed example is not shown, the information known is included in the caption of the photograph, or the reader is referred to Lois Lehner's *Encyclopedia of U.S. Marks on Pottery, Porcelain, & Clay*. For specific information on the American companies who produced the Willow pattern, readers should see Ms. Lehner's book.

The fourth section shows several marks from other countries such as Belgium, France, Sweden, etc. Examples from such countries are not as prolific as those from England, Japan, and the United States, and most were on pieces with the Traditional pattern. Examples were included in the first edition, but most of those have been deleted. The marks are included like the Japanese ones, because the number and variety are interesting to collectors. These marks are arranged alphabetically by country, and are lettered "a," "b," "c," etc. when more than one mark is shown for a country.

W.A. Adderley (a), c. 1876-1885

Adderley (b), c. 1929-1947

Adderley (c), c. after 196 ("Lawley" indicates retaile

Charles Allerton & Sons (a), c. 1890-1912

Charles Allerton & Sons (b), c. 1890-1912

Charles Allerton & Sons (c), c. 1903-1912

Charles Allerton & Sons (d), c. 1929-1942

G.L. Ashworth (a), afte 1880

G.L. Ashworth (b), 20th century

H. Aynsley & Co., c. 1873-1932

Barker Bros. Ltd. (a), marks c 1930-1937 (Godden, Sept. 14, 1987

Barker Bros. Ltd. (b), c. 1930-1937

Booths (a), c. 1906

Booths (b), c. 1912

Bourne & Leigh, c. 1892-1939

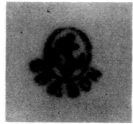

Sampson Bridgwood & Son, c. 1885

Broadhurst & Sons (Crown Pottery), c. 1854-1863 (Godden, June 23, 1987)

Burgess & Leigh (a), c. 1930s and modern

Burgess & Leigh (b), c. 1930s and modern

Burgess & Leigh (c), c. 1930s

Coalport (a), c. 1891-1920

Coalport (b), c. 1960

Copeland & Garrett,
c. 1833-1847

W.T. Copeland &
Sons (a), c. 1883

W.T. Copeland (b),
c. 1875-1890

Crown Stafford-
shire Porcelain
Co., Ltd., c. 1930-
1947

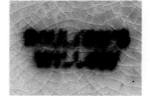

Doulton & Co., Ltd. (a),
c. 1882-1890

Doulton & Co.,
Ltd. (b), c. 1891-
1902

Doulton & Co.,
Ltd. (c), c. after
1891-1902

Royal Doulton (d), c. 1902
(without "Made in Eng-
land"; after 1930 with
"Made in England")

Dudson, Wilcox & Till Ltd., c. 1902-1926

William & Samuel Edge, c. 1841-1847 (Godden,
Sept. 14, 1987)

Edge, Malkin & Co., c. 1873-1903

Gibson & Sons, Ltd., c. 1912-1930

James Green & Newphew Ltd. (no date information, see Godden p. 288 for James Green & Sons; also see Wedgwood & Co. (b) for double mark with this company)

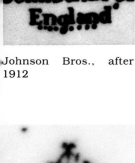

Johnson Bros., after 1912

A.B. Jones & Sons, c. 1900-1913

George Jones & Sons, c. 1924-1951

William Kent, see Godden p. 371

John Maddock, c. 1961

C.T. Maling (a), c. 1875-1908

C.T. Maling (b), c. 1908

C.T. Maling (c), c. 1949-1963

Mason's (a), 19th century mark

Mason's (b), after 1891

Mason's (c), after 1891

Alfred Meakin (a), c. 1930s

Allfred Meakin (b), c. 1930s

J. & G. Meakin, c. 1970s

Charles Meigh & Sons, c. 1851-1861

John Meir & Son, c. 1890-1897

"WILLOW"
W.R. MIDWINTER LTD
ENGLAND

W.R. Midwinter (b), c. 1946

Myott, Son, & Co., c. 1936

W.R. Midwinter, Ltd. (a), after 1932 (Godden, Sept. 14, 1987)

Parrott & Co., c. 1935

Pountney & Co., Ltd. (a), after 1900

Pountney & Co., Ltd. (b), c. 1930s

Pountney & Co., Ltd. (c), c. 1930s

Samuel Radford, c. 1880-1891

Ridgways (a), c. 1927 (Bow and Quiver mark alone with "England" c. 1912-1927)

Ridgways (b), c. 1927

James Sadler & Sons, after 1946

John Steventon & Sons, Ltd. (b), c. 1923-1936

John Steventon & Sons, Ltd. (a), c. 1923-1936

Taylor, Tunnicliffe & Co.,
c. 1875-1898

John Tams Ltd., after 1930

Washington Pottery Ltd.,
after 1946

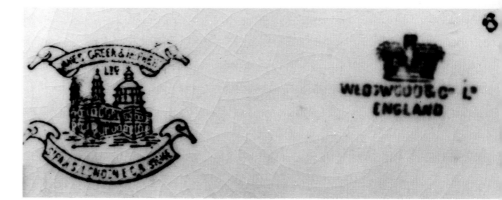

Wedgwood & Co. (b), c. 1906 (double marked with "James Green & Nephew")

Wedgwood & Co. (a),
after 1891.

Wedgwood & Co. (c), c.
1908

Josiah Wedgwood (a), c.
1878

WILLOW
WEDGWOOD
ETRURIA ENGLAND

Josiah Wedgwood (b),
after 1891.

Josiah Wedgwood (c),
modern mark ("circle"
part of mark used after
1940, see Godden
#4099)

Arthur J. Wilkinson (a), c. 1907

Arthur J. Wilkinson, Ltd. (b), c. 1910

H.M. Williamson & Sons, c. 1928-1941

Wood & Sons (a), c. 1907

Wood & Sons, Ltd. (b), c. 1917

Wood & Sons (c), c. early 1900s

Wood & Sons, Ltd. (d), c. 1971 (similar mark used after 1960, see Godden #4297)

Worcester Royal Porcelain Company, (a), c. 1876-1891 ("T" below mark indicates 1882)

Worcester Royal Porcelain Company (b), c. 1940

Unidentified English company (a), Iron Stone China

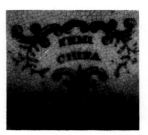

Unidentified English company (b), Semi-China

Unidentified English company (c), Staffordshire Bow Knot

Unidentified English company (d), Stone China

Unidentified English company (e), Old Willow Pattern

Unidentified English company (f), Ye Olde Willow

—— Japanese Marks ——

Nippon, Royal Sometuke (early Noritake), c. 1906

Made in Japan (a), H.B.

Made in Japan (b), House of Blue Willow (same company as "Japan" mark d)

Made in Japan (c), M.D.

Made in Japan (d), Moriyama

Made in Japan (e), Noritake, after 1904

Made in Japan (f), S.P.M.C.

Made in Japan (g), Y.S.

Made in Japan (h), Y.S.

Made in Japan (i), no initials, wreath mark

Made in Japan (j), no initials, flag

Made in Japan (k), no initials, crown

Made in Japan (l), no initials, tulips

Made in Occupied Japan (a), Kakusa China

Made in Occupied Japan (b), Maruta China

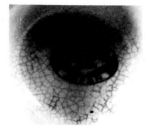

Made in Occupied Japan (c), Morikin Ware

Made in Occupied Japan (d), N.K. Porcelain Co. (Two Phoenix mark)

Made in Occupied Japan (e), no initials, crown

Made in Occupied Japan (f), R.P.

Made in Occupied Japan (g), appears to be N.K. (Two Phoenix mark)

Made in Occupied Japan (h), no initials, wreath and flower.

JAPAN

Japan (a)

Japan (b), Grantcrest

Japan (c), Heirloom

Japan (d), House of Blue Willow (same company as "Made in Japan" mark b)

Japan (e), N.K. Porcelain Co., (Two Phoenix mark)

Japan (f), Royal M by Nikko

Japan (g), Old Tower

Japan (h), Pink Willow

Japan (i), Transor Ware

——— American Marks ———

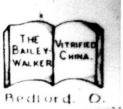

The Bailey-Walker Co., Bedford, Ohio, c. early 1920s-1940

Bennett, Baltimore, Maryland, c. 1930s

Buffalo Pottery (a), Buffalo, New York, c. 1905-1915

Buffalo China (b), after 1915

Carr China, Grafton, West Virginia, 1916-1952 (dates in operation)

Cleveland China, Cleveland, Ohio, before 1940

Hamilton Ross, mark used by an American distributor of china, dates uncertain, probably 1930s-1940s

Ideal, company not identified

Jackson China Company (a), Falls Creek, Pennsylvania, c. 1951

Jackson China Company (b)

Jackson China Company (c), c. 1950s-1960s

Knickerbocker, company unidentified

Edwin M. Knowles, Newell, West Virginia, after 1920

Homer Laughlin (a), East Liverpool, Ohio, mark for April 1964

Homer Laughlin (b), c. early 1940s

Homer Laughlin (c), mark for June 1964

Limoges China Company (a), Sebring, Ohio, before 1955

Limoges China Company (b), before 1955

Nelson McCoy, Roseville, Ohio, after 1940

McNichol China, Clarksburg, West Virginia, c. 1960s

Mayer China, Beaver Falls, Pennsylvania, c. 1918

Paden City Pottery, Paden City, West Virginia, before 1963

Royal China Company (a), Sebring, Ohio, c. 1930s-1940s

Royal China Company (b), c. 1930s-1940s

Royal China Company
(c), c. 1930s-1940s

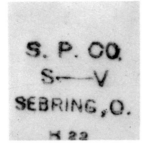

Royal China Company
(d), c. 1930s-1950s

Royal China Company
(e), c. after mid 1960s

E.H. Sebring China
Company, Sebring, Ohio,
before 1935

Sebring Pottery (a), Se-
bring, Ohio, before
1950s

Sebring Pottery (b), be-
fore 1950s

Shenango China (a), New
Castle, Pennsylvania,
before 1968

Shenango China (b)

Sterling China Company (a), East Liverpool, Ohio (offices), c. 1970s

Sterling China
Company (b), c. af-
ter 1950

Sterling China Com-
pany (c), c. 1940s-
1950s

Sterling China Com-
pany (d), c. early
1960s

USA, company not iden-
tified

Walker China Company
(a), Bedford, Ohio, c.
1961

Walker China Company
(b), c. 1969

Wallace China Company
(a), Vernon, California,
before 1964

Wallace China Company
(b), before 1964

Wellsville China, Wells-
ville, Ohio, before 1970

Miscellaneous Foreign Marks

Belgium, Manufacture
Imperial Royale, Nimy,
20th century

Finland, Arabia, after
1948

France (a), Grands Es-
tablissements Cer-
amique Nord, before
1891

France (b), Hamage and
Moulin des Loups, Nord,
after 1891

France (c), Keller and
Guerin, Luneville, after
1891

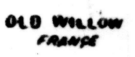

France (d), "Old Willow,"
unidentified company,
after 1891

France (e), "Made in
France," unidentified
company, early 20th
century

Germany, Villeroy &
Boch, Saar Basin, 20th
century

Holland (a), Petrus Regout, Maestricht, before 1891

Holland (b), Societe Ceramique, Maestricht, after 1891

Ireland, Arklow, modern (prior to early 1980's)

Mexico, Anfora, modern

Poland, unidentified company, 20th century

Portugal, Gilman, Sacavem

Sweden, Old Gustavsberg

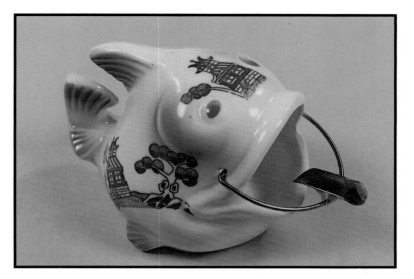

Plate 1. Ashtray, 4"d, advertisement for "Schweppes Table Waters," English, unmarked. *1995 - 35⁰⁰ to 45⁰⁰*

Plate 2. Ashtray, 5"l, fish figure, marked "Japan." (95) *25⁰⁰ to 30⁰⁰*

Plate 3. Ashtray, 7½"sq, Japanese, unmarked. (95) *40⁰⁰ to 45⁰⁰*

Plate 4. Ashtrays 6"l, Traditional border pattern, centers marked "Exclusively for your ashes" and "Cigarettes in here please"; another version (not shown) asks, "Who burnt our tablecloth?"; marked "Japan." (95) *45⁰⁰ to 50⁰⁰ each*

Plate 5. Baking Dish, 2½"h, 5"d, oven proof, marked "Japan."

(95) 30.00 to 35.00

Plate 6. Baking Dish, 3"h, 8"d, Two Temples II Simplified pattern, Line border, American, marked "Hall China."

(95) 25.00 to 30.00

Plate 7. Bank and Planter, 9¼"l, kitten figures, bank unmarked, Japanese; planter marked "Lipper & Mann Inc., Japan."

(95) 250.00 to 275.00 ea

Plate 8. Bank, 7"h, stacked pig figures, Japanese.

(95) 55.00 to 60.00

Plate 9. Batter Jug, 9"h; Syrup, 6"h, frosted glass, plastic lids, American, made by Hazel Atlas Glass Company, marked with raised "H" over "A" trademark.

95   150⁰⁰ to 175⁰⁰ set

Plate 11. Biscuit Jar, 4½", cane handle, Two Temples II pattern, Traditional border, English, Adderley mark b without "Old Willow."

95   175⁰⁰ to 200⁰⁰

Plate 10. Batter Jug, 9½"h; Syrup, 6"h, Japanese, Made in Japan mark d (Moriyama).

95   250⁰⁰ to 300⁰⁰ set

35

Plate 12. Biscuit Jar, cane handle, Made in Japan mark d (Moriyama).

(95) 150⁰⁰ to 175⁰⁰

Plate 13. Biscuit Jar, 6"h, Japanese unmarked, metal handle.

(95) 150⁰⁰ to 175⁰⁰

Plate 14. Biscuit Jar, 7"h, English, unmarked, silver plated lid and bail.

(95) 225⁰⁰ to 250⁰⁰

Plate 15. Biscuit Jar, 6½"h, cane handle, octagonal shape, English, Gibson & Sons, Ltd.

(95) 225⁰⁰ to 250⁰⁰

Plate 16. Bone Dish, 7½"l, 4½"w, English, Wood and Sons mark d.

9 f   45⁰⁰ to 55⁰⁰

Plate 17. Bone Dish, 6¼"l, English, Bourne & Leigh (E.B. & J.E.L.)

45⁰⁰ to 55⁰⁰

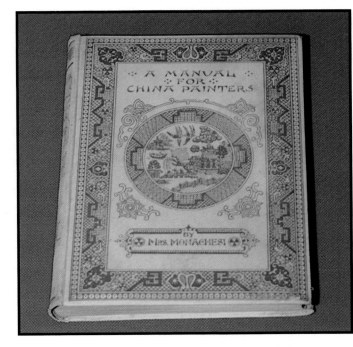

Plate 18. Book, *A Manual for China Painters*, 1897, Traditional pattern on cover.

60⁰⁰ to 75⁰⁰

Plate 19. Bowl, 8½"d, pierced for draining Berries or Cucumbers, with underplate, octagonal shape, English, Josiah Wedgwood mark b.

800⁰⁰ octaware set

Plate 20. Bowl, 15"d, large size for making Bread dough, reversed Traditional center pattern, Japanese, unmarked.

200⁰⁰ to 225⁰⁰

Plate 21. Bowl, 10¼"l, oval shape with reticulated sides, scalloped rim, applied handles, used for holding hot Chestnuts, English creamware, unmarked, ca. early 19th century.

Plate 22. Underplate for Chestnut bowl, 10½"l, reticulated, English, unmarked, ca. early 19th century.

Plate 23. Bowl, 10"l, reticulated sides, for Chestnuts, English, unmarked.

Plate 24. Bowl, 9"d, for Fruit or Berries, scalloped rim, gold trim, silver plated footed holder with handle, Traditional center pattern, Floral and Scroll border pattern, English, W.T. Copeland mark b.

Plate 25. Bowl, 11½"d, shallow bowls of this type are called "Bulb" bowls, lustre multi-colored Traditional pattern, English, S. Fielding Co., Godden Mark 1548.

Plate 26. Bowl, 11"d, 3½"h, Console type, glass, Traditional pattern etched in green enamel, American, made by the Cambridge Glass Co., marked.

Plate 27. Bowl, 9"d, 3½"h, covered, knob handle, this type of bowl is called a "Muffin" dish, English, illegible mark.

Plate 28. Bowl, 9¼"d, 5"h, Pedestal base, English, John Tams Ltd.

Plate 29. Bowl, 7½"d, 4"h, Pedestal base undecorated, Holland mark b with "Willow" (Societe Ceramique).

Plate 30. Bowl, 9"d, 6"h, tall Pedestal base, handles, Punch bowl, English, Josiah Wedgwood mark b.

Plate 31. Bowl, 5¼", 3"h, Rice Bowl, English, Ridgways mark a, Two Temples II reversed pattern, Butterfly border.

Plate 32. Bowl, 9"d, 4"h, Salad Bowl, square shape, English, Ridgways mark a.

Plate 33. Bowl, 10"d, 3½"h, Salad Bowl with fork and spoon, ceramic and wood, Japanese, unmarked.

120⁰⁰ to 140⁰⁰

Plate 34. Salad Fork & Spoon, 11¼"l, ceramic and silver plate, unmarked.

Plate 35. Bowls, Hotel or Restaurant ware for sauces or individual servings: top, 6"l, marked "Higgins & Seiter, England, Hotel Ware"; left, American, marked "Walker China"; right, English, marked "Willow, Wood & Sons, Albert Pick & Co., Chicago."

Plate 36. Bowls, Sauce or individual serving dishes: one handled dish, 7"l; two-handled dish, 8½"l, English, Ridgways mark a.

Plate 37. Bowl, 7½"d, Soup or Cereal, scalloped rim, English, Doulton mark a, Flow Blue Willow.

Plate 38. Bowls, Soup, 7½"d, English, Barker Bros. Ltd., mark a.

Plate 39. Bowls: left, Soup or Cereal; right, individual Custard or Dessert dish, American, Shenango China mark a.

Plate 40. Bowl, Vegetable, oval, 10"l, English, Wood & Sons mark a with pattern name "Hankow" (Booths variant center pattern with border variation), Multicolored Willow.

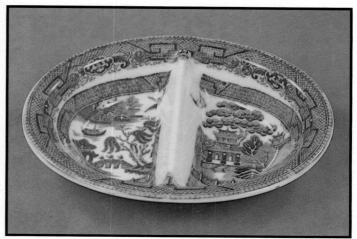

Plate 41. Bowl, Vegetable, oval, divided into four compartments, 13"l, 11"w, English, "Spode" impressed mark, early 19th century.

Plate 42. Bowl, Vegetable, divided, 7¼"l, English, Allerton mark d.

Plate 43. Bowl, Vegetable, 8¾" x 7", English, unmarked.

Plate 44. Bowl, Vegetable, footed, 12¼" x 9½", English, unmarked.

Plate 45, right: Bowl, Vegetable, 11"l, English, Davenport impressed anchor mark, ca. late 18th century, see Godden Mark 1181.

Plate 46, below left: Bowls, Vegetable, round with scalloped edge, 8"d and 10"d, English, Allerton mark a.

Plate 47, below right: Bowl, Vegetable, round with scalloped edge, 9"d, Booths center pattern, Bow Knot border, English, Booths mark b.

Plate 48. Bowl, Vegetable, 10"d, porcelain, Traditional center pattern, Borderless, English, Coalport mark b.

Plate 49. Bowl, Vegetable, 8"d, American, Shenango China mark a.

Plate 50. Bowl, Vegetable, 9¼"d, beaded outer rim, English, Aynsley & Co.

Plate 51. Bowl, Vegetable, 9¾"d, Japanese, Japan mark h, Pink Willow.

Plate 52. Bowl, Vegetable, 8½"d, Simplified Traditional center pattern, Floral border (Bridal Gold #1), American, Hamilton Ross mark with "Ming Red," Red Willow.

Plate 53. Bowl, Vegetable, 10"d, Variant center pattern, Pictorial border, unmarked.

Plate 54. Bowl, Vegetable, porcelain, Pictorial border pattern, Nippon mark (Royal Sometuke).

Plate 55. Bowl, Vegetable, 9¾" square shape, English, unidentified English mark f ("Ye Olde Willow").

Plate 56. Bowl, Vegetable, 8" square shape, English, Booths center pattern, Bow Knot border, Booths mark a.

Plate 57. Bowl, Vegetable, Covered, 8"，3½"h, pierced hole in lid, English, John Tams (Tams Ware).

Plate 58. Lid to Covered Vegetable Bowl, 7½" sq, Burleigh center pattern, Scroll & Flower border, English, unmarked, Multicolored Willow.

Plate 59. Bowl, Vegetable, Covered, 9¼"sq plus handles, 7"h, interior pattern, English, Broadhurst & Sons, Crown Pottery, ca. mid 19th century.

Plate 60. Bowl, Vegetable, Covered, 6" x 12", scalloped edge, interior pattern, English, Allerton mark d, Pink Willow.

Plate 61. Bowl, Vegetable, Covered, 6" x 10", English, Adderley mark b.

Plate 62. Bowl, Vegetable, Covered, 10"d, John Steventon mark b, Mulberry Willow.

Plate 63. Bowl, Vegetable, covered, 9" x 5½" scalloped edge, interior pattern, American, Buffalo Pottery mark a for 1911.

Plate 64. Bowl, Vegetable, Covered, 10½" x 6", unmarked.

Plate 65. Bowls, Vegetable, Covered, Stacked set of 3, 8"l, Made in Japan mark d (Moriyama).

Plate 66. Bowls, Vegetable Covered, Stacked set of 4, 9"d, Made in Japan mark d (Moriyama).

Plate 67. Bowl, Vegetable, Covered, 9½"d, English, Myott, Son & Co., Godden Mark 2811.

Plate 68. Bowl, Vegetable, Covered, 9"d, English, Gibson and Sons, Ltd. without "Willow."

Plate 69. Bowl, Vegetable, Covered, 9"d, marked "Japan."

Plate 70. Bowl, Vegetable, Covered, 10"d, English, W.R. Midwinter, Ltd., mark a.

Plate 71. Bowl, Vegetable, Covered, 9"d, interior pattern, English, marked "Grimwades, Upper Hanley Pottery."

Plate 72. Bowl, Vegetable, Covered, 11½"d, porcelain, Mandarin pattern, Dagger border, pierced handles and finial, English, Copeland, Godden Mark 1073, impressed mark for 1880.

Plate 73. Bowl, Vegetable, Covered, Divided, 11½"d, Mandarin pattern, Dagger border, two lids, applied flower and stem finials on lids, English, "Copeland" impressed mark, ca. late 1880s.

Plate 74. Bowl, Vegetable, Covered, 11" x 8½", Variant pattern decals on sides of bowl and around lid, American, Limoges China Company.

Plate 75. Bowl, Vegetable, Covered, 11½" x 9", Worcester pattern, Scroll and Flower border, English, Pountney & Co., Ltd., Godden Mark 3113, Gray-Green Willow.

Plate 76. Bowl, Tureen with ladle, 15" x 11", Unidentified English mark a.

Plate 77. Bowl, Tureen with ladle, 9" x 6", English, unmarked.

Plate 78. Bowl, Tureen, English, marked "Semi-China" in a square, unidentified company.

Plate 79. Bowl, Tureen, 10" x 6", scalloped footed base, Japanese, unmarked.

Plate 80. Bowl, Tureen, Sauce, 4½"h, with Tray, 5" x 7", English, marked "G. Phillips, Longport," ca. mid 19th century.

Plate 81. Bowl, Tureen, Sauce, 7"d, ladle, interior pattern, unmarked.

Plate 82. Butter Dish, Covered, 8"d, 3"h, unidentified English mark f.

Plate 83. Butter Dish, Covered, 4½"h, Two Temples II pattern on base, silver lid with cow finial and Traditional inner border pattern, silver interior liner, English, unmarked.

Plate 84. Butter Dish, Covered, 8"d, 3½"h, English, Josiah Wedgwood mark b.

Plate 85. Butter Dish, Covered, holds one quarter pound, marked "Japan."

Plate 86. Butter Dish, Covered, 6"l, holds one-quarter pound, marked "Japan."

Plate 87. Butter Dish, 6½"d, open style with "Butter" embossed on side, Traditional center pattern, Butterfly border, unmarked.

Plate 88. Butter Dish, 6"d (including wooden holder), English, George Jones & Sons, see Godden Mark 2218.

Plate 89. Butter Pats, from top and left to right: 3", English, Myott, Son, and Co.; 3", unmarked; 3½", marked "England"; 3½", marked "England"; 3", marked "Made in Japan"; 3", marked "England."

Plate 90, above left: Butter Warmer, Japanese, unmarked.

Plate 91, above right: Candelabra, 11"h, brass and ceramic, matching side dishes, American, Shenango China mark a.

Plate 92, left: Candle Holders, 5½"h, Two Temples II Simplified pattern, Pictorial border, unmarked, Multi-colored Willow.

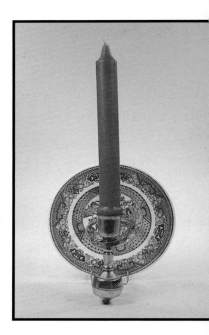

Plate 93, left: Candle Holders, 7½"h, English Doulton mark b, Flow Blue Willow.

Plate 94, right: Candle Holder, Ship's Light, brass with ceramic backplate, unmarked.

Plate 95. Candle Holder, Chamber-stick type, 5"d, scalloped edge, gold trim, English, Gibson & Sons.

Plate 96. Cannister Set: Flour, Sugar, Coffee, and Tea in graduated sizes, barrel shape, Japanese.

Plate 97. Cannister Set: Flour, 7"h; Sugar, 5½"h; Coffee, 5"h; Tea, 4½"h; square shape, tin, unmarked.

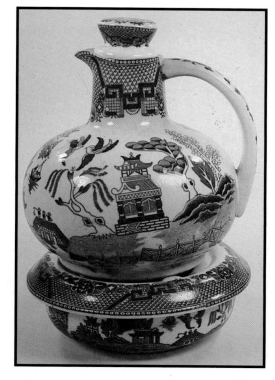

Plate 98. Carafe and Warmer, 10"h overall, marked "Japan."

Plate 99. Cheese Dish, English, Wiltshaw & Robinson, Godden Mark 4201 (Carlton Ware).

Plate 100. Cheese Dish, Burleigh pattern, Scroll and Flower border, English, Burgess & Leigh mark a (Burleigh Ware).

Plate 101. Cheese & Cracker Dish, 10"d, enamelled pattern, gold trim, American, Cambridge Glass Company, unmarked.

Plate 102. Child's Toy Tea Dishes: Covered Sugar, 3½"h; Saucer, 4½"d; Cup, 1½"h; Mandarin pattern, Dagger border, English, marked "Copeland," Pink Willow.

Plate 103. Child's Covered Butter Dish, 5½"d, English, Edge, Malkin & Co.

Plate 104. Child's Tea Cup, 1½"h; Saucer, 3¼"d, unmarked, Japanese, Brown Willow.

Plate 105. Child's Toy Dishes: Grill Plate, ½"d; Cake Plate, 5"d; marked "Made in Japan"; Tin Plate, 1½"d, unmarked.

Plate 106. Child's Toy Dishes: porcelain, Tea Set for 6 with covered Vegetable, Platter (or under plate), and Gravy dish marked "Japan."

400^{00} to 300^{00}

Plate 107. Child's Toy Dishes: Platter, Gravy and Underplate, Covered Vegetable Bowl and Underplate; English, Ridgways mark a.

Plate 108. Child's Toy Tea Set: tin, ca. late 1940s American, Ohio Art Co.

Plate 109. Child's Toy Tea Set: plastic, original box, American, Ideal Toys.

Plate 110. Child's Toy Tea Set: plastic, 15 pieces, Traditional center pattern, Butterfly border, American, Ideal Toys.

Plate 111. Chocolate Set: Pot, 8"h, Cups, 3"h, Two Temples II pattern, Butterfly border, English, marked "Hammersley's China, England" and "Pitkin & Brooks, Chicago."

Plate 112. Cigar Lighter, metal stand and fittings, metal marked "B. & Co. London," but china is unmarked.

Plate 113. Clock, 8 Day, German works, tin, Pictorial border, Traditional pattern.

Plate 114. Clock, tin, marked "Smith's, Made in Great Britain."

Plate 115. Coaster, (also called Tip Trays), 4"d, advertisement for "Yorkshire Relish," English, unmarked.

Plate 116. Coaster, 4"d, advertisement for "Tennent's Pilsener Beer," English, unmarked.

Plate 117. Coasters: left, 4"d, ceramic dish in wooden and metal holder, English, George Jones & Son; right, 4"d, ceramic dish in wooden holder, green painted border, English, unmarked.

Plate 118. Cocktail Shaker, 12"h overall, 6 matching Tumblers, 3"h, clear glass with metal lid for shaker, American, Hazel Atlas.

Plate 119. Coffee Jar, 6"h, for instant coffee, marked "Japan."

Plate 120. Coffee Jar, 6"h, for instant coffee, plastic measuring spoon and holder on side of jar, Japanese, unmarked.

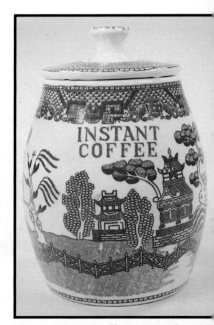

Plate 121. Coffee Jar, for instant coffee, unmarked, Japanese.

Plate 122. Coffee Pot, 7"h, marked "Japan."

Plate 123. Coffee Pot, 6½"h, granite ware, unmarked.

Plate 124. Coffee Pot, 6"h, granite ware, unmarked.

Plate 125. Coffee Urn and revolving Serving Tray, 17"d, pedestal base, 4¼"h, Two Temples I pattern on Urn, Two Temples II pattern on tray, porcelain, English, W.T. Copeland, Godden Mark 1073, impressed mark for 1883.

Plate 126. Comb Holder, 6½"h, 4½"w pierced for hanging, English registr mark, Red Willow.

Plate 127. Compote, 3½"h, 9"d, English, Doulto mark c, Flow Blue Willow.

Plate 128. Compote, 4¼"h, 10"l, oval shape, "Laxton Cambridge" printed below birds in center pattern, English, unmarked.

Plate 129. Compote, 3"h, 6"d, American, Shenango China mark a.

Plate 132. Condiment Cruet Set: Holder, 7½"h overall fitted with Oil, Vinegar, Pepper, Salt, and Mustard Cruets, marked "Japan."

Plate 130. Compote, 3½"h, 11"l, oval shape, earthenware, English, Spode, ca. late 18th century, see Godden Mark 3648. The pattern is Spode's Willow I.

Plate 131. Compote, 8"d, Mandarin pattern, Dagger border, earthenware, English, Copeland, impressed mark before 1891.

Plate 133. Condiment Set: wood and ceramic, Salt and Pepper Shakers, covered Mustard, two drawers in base, Japanese.

Plate 134. Condiment Cruet Set made in figural form, each approximately 5"h: Mustard, Pepper, Vinegar, Open Salt; Traditional border pattern, English, unmarked. These are commonly referred to as "Prestopans" because they were made by potteries in Prestopan, Scotland during the early to mid 1800s.

Plate 135. Condiment Set: tray, 6"l, clover leaf shape fitted with Pepper Pot, Open Salt, and Mustard Pot (without lid), unidentified English mark e (Old Willow Pattern).

Plate 136, left: Condiment Set: Stand, 3½"d, 4½"h overall, metal fitted with Pepper Pot, Mustard Pot, and Open Salt Dish; Two Temples II pattern, Borderless, English, Taylor, Tunnicliffe & Co.

Plate 137, above: Condiment Shaker, 2"h, pierced silver lid, English, Taylor, Tunnicliffe & Co.

Plate 138. Cookie Jar, 9"h, made in form of a pitcher, American, McCoy.

50⁰⁰ to 6⁰⁰ Lid too

Plate 139. Cook Ware (set includes a 10" Skillet not shown), American, General Housewares.

Plate 140. Cow figure, 7½"l, 6"h, with milkmaid seated on stool, English Staffordshire figures, 19th century, unmarked.

Plate 141. Creamer, Cow figure, 7"l, 5"h, fitted with stopper, English, unmarked.

Plate 142. Creamers, Cow figures: left to right; 7"l; 7"l; 6¾"l; 6½"l; English, all unmarked except one on right end has William Kent's mark, see Godden Mark 2272, ca. mid 1900s.

Plate 143. Creamers, individual size, hotel ware, ranging from 1½"h to 2¼"h, front to back: English, Maddock; bisque, unmarked; American, Buffalo China; Buffalo China; Walker China; Shenango China; Shenango China.

Plate 144. Creamer, individual size, 2"h, scalloped edge, marked "England."

Plate 145. Creamer, individual size, 2½"h, hotel ware, American, Shenango China mark a.

Plate 146, above left: Creamer, 3"h, hotel ware, American, Buffalo China mark for 1922.

Plate 147, above right: Creamer, 3"h, porcelain, Pictorial border, Traditional pattern, gold trim, marked "Willow" in gold with number "6333," Multi-colored Willow.

Plate 148, right: Creamer, 3½"h, Japanese, Made in Japan mark h.

Plate 149. Creamer, 2½"h, American, unmarked.

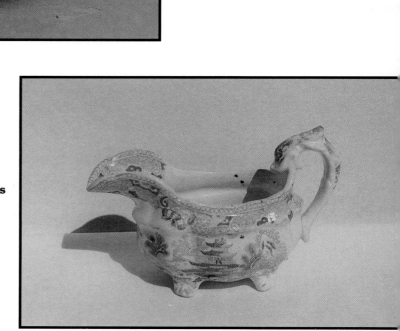

Plate 150. Creamer, 4"h, 6"l, footed, Two Temples II pattern, Butterfly border, unmarked.

Plate 151. Creamer, 2"h, Turner pattern, Scroll and Flower border, English, marked "Royal Worcester Crown Willow."

Plate 152. Creamer, 3"h; Sugar Bowl, 5½"h; English, marked "Bakewell Bros.," see Godden Mark 236.

Plate 153. Creamer & Sugar Bowl, 3½"h, gold trim, unmarked, Japanese.

Plate 154. Creamer & Sugar Bowl, 5"h, Canton pattern, English, G.L. Ashworth mark b.

Plate 155. Creamer, 3"h; Sugar Bowl, 4"h, English, John Steventon & Sons mark a.

Plate 156. Crisper, 10"h, marked "Blue Magic Krispy Kan, The Luce Corp., South Norwalk, Conn."

Plate 157. Cup, oversize for Chili, 4"h, 4½"d, Japanese, unmarked.

Plate 158, above: Cups, 2¼"h and 2½"h, called "Coffee Cans" because of their straight cylinder shape, Two Temples II pattern reversed, Butterfly border, English, unmarked.

Plate 159, left: Cup, 3"h, short pedestal base, used for serving custard, American, Homer Laughlin, unmarked.

Plate 160. Cups, Demi-tasse, 2½"h and Saucers, Pictorial border, restaurant ware, American, Buffalo China.

14⁰⁰ to 18⁰⁰

Plate 161, left: Cup, Demi-tasse, 2½"h, Saucer, 4½"d, marked "Japan."

Plate 162, below, Cup, Demi-tasse, and Saucer, marked "Hand-painted in Occupied Japan," Multicolored Willow.

Plate 163. Cup, demi-tasse and Saucer, Two Temples I pattern, Butterfly border, porcelain, English, Copeland, see Godden Mark 1073, impressed mark for 1878.

Plate 164. Cup, Demi-tasse, 2"h and Saucer, porcelain, Worcester pattern, Scroll and Flower border, gold trim, English, Worcester mark a with "V" and "X" indicating years 1884-1886.

Plate 165. Cup, Demi-tasse and Saucer, Polychrome Variant pattern, black underglaze, English, Crown Staffordshire Porcelain Co., see Godden Mark 1149.

Plate 166. Cup, Handleless, and Saucer, unmarked, Pink Willow.

Plate 167. Cup, Handleless, 2"h, Saucer, 4"d, Mandarin pattern, Traditional border, English, H. Aynsley & Co.

Plate 168. Cup, Handleless, 3½"d, English, Pountney & Co. mark b (Bristol Pottery).

Plate 169. Cup, Handleless, 2½"h, Two Temples II pattern reversed, Butterfly border, English, unmarked.

Plate 170. Cup, Measuring, ceramic with wooden handle, one of four made to fit matching rack, unmarked, Japanese.

Plate 171. Cups, Mugs, 4"h, called "Farmer's Cup" because of large size and heavy construction, marked "Japan." *35⁰⁰ to 40⁰⁰ ea*

Plate 172, above left: Cup, Mug, 3½"h, Japanese, unmarked.

Plate 173, above right: Cup, Mug, 3¾"h, American, USA mark.

Plate 174, right: Cup, Mug, 3½"h, Two Temples II pattern, Line border, hotel ware, American, Sebring Pottery mark b.

Plate 175. Cups, Mugs, 3"h, milk glass with silk-screened pattern, American, "Fire King" made by Anchor Hocking Glass Company.

Plate 176, above left: Cup, Mug, 4"h, Polychrome Variant pattern, full figure in foreground, gold lustre on black background, English, unmarked, mid to late 19th century.

Plate 177, above right: Cup, Mug, "Mother" printed between birds on interior, Japanese, unmarked.

Plate 178, left: Cup, Mustache, 2"h, 4"d, gold trim, English, Minton, see Godden Mark 2713 with "England."

Plate 179, left: Cup, Punch, 3"h, pedestal foot, Two Temples II pattern, Butterfly border, English, unmarked.

Plate 180, below: Cup, Tea, 3"h and Saucer, Mandarin pattern, Dagger border, English, W.T. Copeland & Sons mark a.

Plate 181, above: Cup, Tea and Saucer, "Auld Lang Syne" verse printed around interior rim, English, marked "Copeland," Rust-Orange Willow.

Plate 182, right: Cup, Tea, 1½"h and Saucer, called a 4 o'clock tea cup because of its small height, English, Ridgways mark a.

Plate 183. Cup, 3¼"h and Saucer, "Father" printed between two birds on interior rim, marked "Japan."

Plate 184. Cup, Tea, 4¾"h, English, John Meir & Son.

Plate 185. Cup, 3"h and Saucer, English, Washington Pottery.

Plate 186. Cup, Tea, 2¼"h and Saucer, marked "Made in Japan," Red Willow.

Plate 187. Cup, Tea, 2¼"h, porcelain, Two Temples II pattern, Butterfly border, gold trim, English, W.A. Adderley mark c.

Plate 188. Cup, Tea, 3"h, Two Temples II reversed pattern, Butterfly border, marked "56," no manufacturer's mark.

Plate 189. Cup, Tea, 3"h, porcelain, Pictorial border pattern, Made in Japan mark e (Noritake).

Plate 190. Cup, Tea, 3"h, Polychrome Variant pattern, marked "Made in Occupied Japan."

Plate 191, above: Cup, 5½"h, 8½"d, called a "Texas Cup" because of its large size, marked "Japan."

Plate 192, right: Cup, 4½"h, Two-Handled with Cover, a Cream Soup or Porridge dish, English, Josiah Wedgwood mark b.

Plate 193. Cup, 2½"h, 6½"d, Two-Handled, Cream Soup, unmarked.

Plate 194. Cup, 2½"h, 6"d, Two-Handled, Cream Soup, English, Ridgways mark b.

Plate 195. Cup, 2½"h, 4"d, Two-Handled, Cream
oup, English, John Maddock.

Plate 196. Cup, 3"h, Two-Handled, Cream Soup, Canton
pattern, English, Wood & Sons mark b.

late 197. Cuspidor, 7½"h, large rounded body,
English, Doulton mark b.

Plate 198. Drainers: Butter, left, 3½"d, right, 6"sq,
English, unmarked; back, Meat Drainer, 6"sq, English, unmarked.

Plate 199. Drainer, Meat, 14¼"l, 10¼"w, Turner Center pattern, English, unmarked.

Plate 200. Drainer, Meat, 10"l, 7¼"w, Marked "Iron Stone China," English.

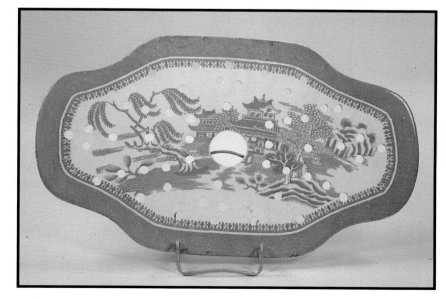

Plate 201. Drainer, Meat, 16"l, Mandarin pattern, Dagger border, English, unmarked.

Plate 202. Dresser Boxes; Left, 1¾"h, 3½"d; right, 2"h, 4"d, porcelain, English, ca. late 1880s, unmarked.

Plate 203. Dresser Box, 3"h, 6"l, Two Temples II pattern reversed, Butterfly border, Minton, see Godden Mark 2713 with "England."

Plate 204. Egg Cups, single type, 1½" to 2"h: left, pedestal base, Japanese; right, gold rim, English, Burleigh Ware; others unmarked. 25⁰⁰ to 35⁰⁰

Plate 205. Egg Cups for Coddled Eggs, 4"h, metal tops, Worcester pattern, Scroll and Flower border, English, Worcester mark b.

Plate 206. Egg Cups, left to right, double type, 3½"h, Two Temples II pattern reversed, Butterfly border, unmarked; 4"h, Booths pattern, Bow Knot border, gold trim, English, Booths mark b; 3½"h, unmarked.

Plate 207. Egg Cups, double type: left, 4½"h, English, marked "Allertons Made in England"; right, 3¾"h, Japanese, unmarked.

Plate 208, left: Egg Stand, silver, fitted with spoon holder, holds eight cups, those shown are single style with pedestal base, porcelain, Traditional center pattern, Variant border, English, marked "Copeland China," see Godden Mark 1077. (Complete with "willowed" eggs!)

Plate 209, above: Egg Stand, 9½"l, 4"h, fitted with salt dip and pierced slots for spoons, English, unmarked.

Plate 210. Fish Platter, 20½"l,   11½"w, gold trim, English Minton, see Godden Mark 2711, year cypher is for 1880.

Plate 211. Fish Serving Knife & Fork, electroplated nickel silver with porcelain handles, English, original case.

Plate 212, left: Flatware, 4 piece place setting, plastic and stainless steel, Japanese.

Plate 213, right: Ginger Jar, 5"h, 4"w, unmarked.

Plate 214. Ginger Jar, 5¼"h, Traditional center pattern, Variant border, English, Pountney & Co. mark c (Bristol Pottery), Rust-Orange Willow.

Plate 215. Ginger Jar, 9"h, Turner center pattern, Scroll and Flower border, English, Mason's mark c, Pink Willow.

Plate 216. Ginger Jar, 5½"h, unmarked.

Plate 217. Ginger Jar, 5"h, English, marked "Arthur Wood, England."

Plate 218. Glasses, ceramic Juice Tumblers, 3½"h, marked "Japan."

Plate 219. Glasses, ceramic, Juice Tumblers, Japanese, unmarked.

Plate 220. Glasses, clear glass Tumblers: left, 5"h; right, 3"h.

Plate 221. Glass, 4"h, flared shape, round foot, enamelled pattern, gold trim, American, Cambridge Glass Co., unmarked, ca. 1929.

Plate 222. Glasses, frosted glass, assorted sizes from 3" to 5¼"h, unmarked.

Plate 223. Glasses, clear glass, 3"h to 4"h, American (left tumbler, c. 1949, made by Jeannette Glass, unmarked; middle tumbler has Libby Glass mark; right tumbler is unmarked).

Plate 224. Glasses, clear glass, 4"h to 5"h, unmarked.

Plate 225. Glasses, 8"h, Pitcher, 10"h, carnival-type glass, American, Jeannette Glass, c. 1949.

[handwritten notes:] f dishes 120⁰⁰ to 140⁰⁰ Glasses 35⁰⁰ to 45⁰⁰ each

Plate 226. Gravy Boat with attached Underplate, 7½"l overall, scalloped edge, English,
Allerton mark d.

Plate 227. Gravy Dish with attached Underplate, 6½"d overall, scalloped edge, English, Dudson, Wilcox, & Till.

Plate 228. Gravy Boat, 8"l, English, Ridgways mark a.

Plate 229. Gravy Dish, 6"d, spout on either side,
"Gravy" and "Lean" printed inside dish, unmarked.

Plate 230. Gray Boat, 7"l, English, Woo
& Sons mark d.

Plate 231. Gravy Boat, 8¾"l, Traditional
pattern with border variation, English,
Arthur J. Wilkinson, Multi-colored Willow.

Plate 232. Gravy Boat, 6"l, Ameri
can, Shenango China mark a.

Plate 233. Honey Dish, 4"d, English, W.R. Midwinter mark b.

Plate 234. Horseradish Dish, 5½"h, English, Doulton mark d.

Plate 235. Hot Pot, 6"h, borderless, marked "Japan."

Plate 236. Hot Pot, 6"h, marked "Japan."

Plate 237. Humidor, 5"h, Worcester Variant pattern, gold trim, English, Wiltshaw & Robinson (Carlton Ware), see Godden Mark 4201, ca. 1900, Flow Blue Willow.

Plate 238. Humidor, 6½"h, English, marked "Doulton, England, Willow," similar to Doulton mark a, gold trim, Brown Willow.

Plate 239. Inkwells, double style, 8½"l, 2¼"h, English, Booths similar to mark a (Traditional pattern).

Plate 240. Infant Feeder, 4"h, English, unmarked.

Plate 241. Invalid Feeder, (or libation cup), 2½"h, 6"l, 2"w, English, Wood & Sons, similar to mark c.

Plate 242. Invalid Feeder, Variant pattern, Scroll and Flower border, English, "Spode" printed in blue, early 19th century.

Plate 243. Jam Dish, individual size, restaurant ware, English, Wood & Sons mark d.

Plate 244. Jam Jar, 7"h, Mandarin pattern, Dagger border, English, W.T. Copeland mark b.

Plate 245. Jardiniere, 4½"h, 8"d, English, John Tams Ltd. (Tams Ware).

Plate 246. Jardiniere, 8½"h, 7"d, English, unmarked.

Plate 247. Jardiniere, 6"h, 7"d, English, Minton, see Godden Marks 2713 and 2714, ca. 1900, Flow Blue Willow.

Plate 248. Juicer or Reamer, 6"h, 7"w, Japanese, Made in Japan mark d (Moriyama).

Plate 249. Knife Rest, 4"l, Traditional border pattern, English, unmarked.

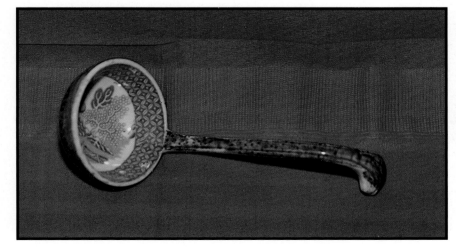

Plate 250. Ladle, 8"l, Traditional center pattern, unmarked.

Plate 251. Ladles: 12¼"l; 7"l, unmarked.

Plate 252. Lamp, 8"h, Kerosene, with Reflector, Japanese.

Plate 253, left: Lamp, 7¼"h, Electric made in Oil Lamp style, marked, "Made in Japan."

Plate 254, above: Lamps, Kerosene, ceramic shades: 8"h, 8½"h, 11½"h; Japanese.

Plate 255, right: Lamp Base, 9"h, unmarked, Green Willow.

Plate 256, below left: Lamp Base, 12"h, mounted on brass stand, decorated finial, English, mark not visible.

Plate 257, below right: Lamp Base, 10"h, mounted on brass stand, English, Wedgwood & Co., see Godden mark 4056, Red Willow.

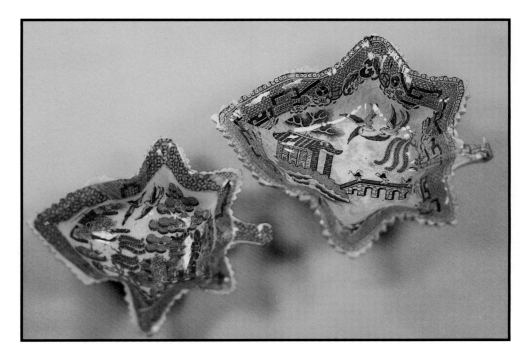

Plate 258. Leaf Dishes: 5½"l, 6"l; English, unmarked (also called Nut or Pickle dishes).

Plate 259. Mantle Set: pair of plates (see following photograph) fitted with a portrait and a clock; 8"d, ruffled rim, gold trim and gold spattered work, brass frames, English, Doulton mark a (clock made by British United Clock Co.).

Plate 260. Matching Plate of Doulton Mantle Set.

Plate 261. Matches in box with Simplified Traditional pattern. "Made exclusively for Freund, Mayer, & Co., Inc., New York," and "Made in Italy," printed on bottom of box.

Plate 262. Match Safe, 2"h, American, Shenango China Co. mark b.

Plate 263. Muffineer, also called a Sugar Shaker (American term), or a Pepper Pot (English term), 5"h, marked "Made in Japan."

Plate 264. Muffineer, 5½"h, octagonal body shape, unmarked.

90⁰⁰ to 95⁰⁰

Plate 265. Muffineer, 7"h, Simplified Two Temples II pattern reversed, Line border, metal top, English, marked "Lancaster Ltd. Hanley, England," mark is after 1906.

Plate 266. Mustard Pot, 3½"h, Two Temples II Simplified pattern, Pictorial border, metal lid, English, Parrott and Co., Multi-colored willow.

Plate 267. Mustard Pot, 2½"h, flared neck, handle, unmarked.

Plate 269. Mustard Pot, 2½"h, barrel shape, unmarked.

Plate 268. Mustard Pot, 2½"h, American, Shenango China mark a.

Plate 270. Napkin Ring, 1½"l, unmarked.

Plate 271. Necklace Pendant, 2¾"d, brass framed back, Advertisement for "Manchester Tailoring Depot, Bolton" on front; a "Gentlemen's" clothing store on back (see following photograph), English, unmarked.

Plate 272. Back of Necklace in preceding photograph.

Plate 273. Oil & Vinegar Set, bottles, 6"h, Japanese.

Plate 274. Oil & Vinegar Set, bottle with double spout, made for wooden rack with holders for a Funnel and Salad Fork and Spoon, Japanese.

Plate 275. Pepper Mill, 3¾"h, Traditional center pattern, Variant border on base, unmarked.

Plate 276. Pepper Mill, 3"h, metal top and grinder, unmarked, Brown Willow with lustre finish.

Plate 277. Pepper Pot (or Muffineer), 3¾"h, rounded body and top, short pedestal foot, unmarked.

Plate 278. Perfume Bottle with stopper, 6"h, Mandarin pattern, Dagger border, English, marked "Copeland."

Plate 279. Perfume Bottle, 1⅝"l, silve top, English, Worcester mark a fo 1884.

Plate 281. Pie Server or Pastry Knife, 10"l, Japanese, Made in Japan mark d (Moriyama).

Plate 280. Pie Plate, 10"d, unglazed base for baking, Japanese, Made in Japan mark d (Moriyama).

Plate 282. Pitcher, 7"h, Booths pattern, Bow Knot border, gold trim, English, Booths mark b.

125.00 to 150.00

Plate 283. Pitcher, 5"h, Mandarin pattern, Dagger border, English, Edge, Malkin, & Co.

Plate 284. Pitcher, 5"h, Turner pattern, Scroll and Flower border, English, Mason mark b, Multi-colored Willow.

Plate 285. Pitchers, 6"h; 5"h, scalloped borders, English, Allerton mark d.

Plate 286. Pitchers, 3 pint size, called "Chicago Jugs": left, American, Buffalo Pottery mark for 1907; right, English, Doulton mark b.

Plate 287. Pitcher, 7"h, English, Doulton mark b.

Plate 288. Pitcher, 7"h, flared spout and base, English, Doulton mark b, Flow Blue Willow.

Plate 289. Pitcher, 6"h, triangular shape, English, Doulton mark b.

Plate 290. Pitcher, 5½"h, porcelain, scalloped neck, English, A.B. Jones & Sons "Grafton China," see Godden Mark 2196.

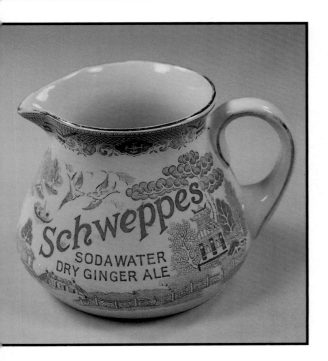

Plate 291. Pitcher, 4"h, Advertisement for Schweppes "Soda Water, Dry Ginger Ale," English, James Green and Nephew.

Plate 292. Pitcher, 8¾"h, Water Pitcher size, English, Ridgways mark a (Bow and Quiver mark only).

Plate 293. Pitcher, 8"h, Simplified Traditional pattern on body, Pictorial border pattern, unmarked.

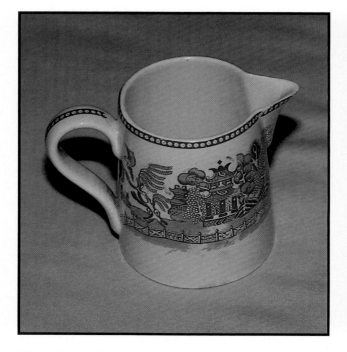

Plate 294. Pitcher, 3¾"h, Holland mark b (Societie Ceramique), Red Willow.

Plate 295. Pitcher, 6"h, English, Johnson Bros., Red Willow

Plate 296. Pitcher, 5½"h, 6"d, English, Ridgways, similar to Godden Mark 3310, ca. 1890s (Godden, September, 1987).

Plate 297. Pitcher, 7"h, English, Josiah Wedgwood mark b, Multicolored Willow.

Plate 298. Pitcher, 4½"h, Two Temples II pattern, Butterfly border, gold band and ring border on neck, English, marked "Semi-China Mfg. for F. Crook, Motcomb St., Belgrave Sq., S.W."

Plate 299. Pitcher, 10"h, Two Temples II Simplified pattern, Pictorial border, English, marked "Morley-Fox," ca. 1920-1930, Multi-colored Willow.

Plate 300, above: Pitcher, 4¾"h, Two Temples II pattern reversed, Butterfly border, English, stamped "Wedgwood & Co. Ltd."

Plate 301, right: Pitcher, 7"h, fitted with pewter lid, Burleigh pattern, Scroll and Flower border, English, Burgess & Leigh mark a (Burleigh Ware).

Plate 302, above left: Pitcher, 9¾"h, twisted rope-style handle, Two Temples II pattern, Butterfly border, unmarked.

Plate 303, above right: Place Card Holder, 3½"d, English, unmarked (a paper card fits behind plate).

Plate 304, right: Place Cards, 2¾"d, pink and blue with undecorated space for writing name, English, Registry marks ca. 1860.

Plate 305. Place Setting, Booths pattern, Bow Knot border, gold trim: Dinner Plate, Salad Plate, Bread & Butter Plate; Fruit Dish and underplate; Cup and Saucer, English, Booths mark b.

Plate 306. Place Setting, English, Allerton mark d on all pieces except Butter Pat which has Allerton mark a, scalloped edge, Traditional center and border patterns: Dinner Plate, Luncheon Plate, Salad Plate, Soup Bowl, Bread & Butter Plate; Cereal Bowl, Fruit Bowl; Individual Butter Pat; Cup & Saucer (small and large).

Plate 307. Place Setting, octagonal shape, Booths Variant pattern, English, J. & G. Meakin (made especially for Neiman Marcus and sold by catalog ca. mid 1970s), Green Willow: Dinner Plate, Salad Plate, Soup/Cereal Bowl, Cup and Saucer.

Plate 308. Place Setting, American, Shenango China mark a, Traditional center and border pattern: Dinner Plate, Bread & Butter plate; Dessert or Fruit Bowl; Cup and Saucer.

Plate 309. Plate 7¾"d, Advertising, "Ye Olde Cheshire Cheese, 145 Fleet Street, Wine Office Court" (a London Pub & Restaurant), Traditional pattern, English, Wedgwood & Co., mark b with James Green & Nephew (for printed part of plate).

Plate 310. Plate, 7"d, Advertising, "My Goodness, My Guiness" (English Beer), Traditional pattern, English, variation of Washington Pottery's "Old Willow" mark.

Plate 311. Plate, 8¾"d, Advertising, "Wallace Q. & S. Store, Lowest Possible Prices, Consistent with Quality," Two Temples II, Reversed, Simplified center pattern, Line border, American, unmarked, attributed to Southern Potteries' Blue Ridge Line, colonial shape.

Plate 312. Plate, Cake, 8½"sq, porcelain, Mandarin center pattern, Dagger border, English, W.T. Copeland & Sons, see Godden Mark 1077, impressed date for 1891.

Plate 313. Plate, Cake, 9½"sq, Mandarin center pattern, Dagger border, English, Shore & Coggins, see Godden Mark 3525.

Plate 314. Plate, Cake, 11"d, two-handled, domed shaped cover, Traditional pattern, Made in Japan, mark d (Moriyama).

Plate 315. Plate, Cake Stand, 4"h, 10½"d, Traditional pattern, English, unmarked.

Plate 316. Plate, Cake or Tea serving plate, two handled, Traditional pattern, English, Unidentified English mark e (Old Willow).

Plate 317. Plate, 12"d, scalloped edge, porcelain, Traditional pattern, English, "Minton" impressed, see Godden mark 2706, ca. 1860s.

Plate 318. Plate, Cake or Tea, 9"d, two handled, Two Temples II center pattern, Butterfly border, unmarked.

Plate 319. Plate, Cake on pedestal stand, 10"d, porcelain, scalloped edge, Worcester pattern, Scroll and Flower border, English, Royal Worcester, see Godden Mark 4354 (the Worcester mark has ten dots indicating a date of 1901).

Plate 320. Plate, Charger or Chop, 13"d, American, Buffalo China mark for 1917, Traditional pattern.

Plate 321. Plate, Charger or Chop, 12¼"d, Traditional pattern, American Royal China Company mark d.

Plate 322. Plate, Collector, 6"d, English, Josiah Wedgwood mark c (without "Willow"), issued in 1971 portraying a scene from "The Sandman," a fairy tale by Hans Christian Andersen incorporating part of the Traditional center pattern.

Plate 323. Plate, Collector, 8¼"d, "Breakfast with Teddy," by illustrator Jesse Wilcox Smith for Hoyle Products. Dishes with the Canton pattern are featured, American.

Plate 324. Plate, Collector, 10½"d, number 3 in a series of plates relating the Willow Story, issued by Royal Doulton from 1920 to 1945. The center pattern portrays one part of the story (see the following photograph); cameos around the border are from other plates in the series.

Plate 325. Plate, back of plate in preceding photograph describing center pattern.

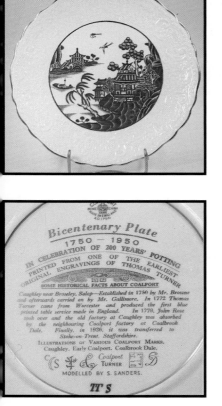

Plate 326, above left: Plate, Commemorative, 9½"d, Bicentenary Plate, English, Coalport, see following photograph.

Plate 327, left: Back of Bicentenary Plate.

Plate 328, above right: Crescent Shaped Plate, 9¼"l, porcelain, partial Traditional center pattern with wide basketweave border, English, T.C. Brown-Westhead, Moore & Co., see Godden Mark 677, 19th century.

Plate 329. Plate, 6"d, English, Booths Variant center pattern, basket-weave type border, English, made by Wood & Sons, see Godden Mark 4291 (with "Hankow" as pattern name), Multi-colored Willow.

Plate 330. Plate, 8¾"d, octagonal shape, Booths Variant center pattern, Bow Knot border, gold trim, English, Booths mark a.

Plate 331. Plate, 10"d, Burleigh center pattern, Scroll and Flower border, English, Burgess & Leigh mark b.

Plate 332. Plate, 9"d, Canton pattern, English, G.L. Ashworth mark b.

Plate 333. Plate, 10½"d, Canton pattern, American, Shenango China Co., marked with date code for 1960.

Plate 334. Plates, 7¾"d 9½"d, Canton pattern American, Syracuse China

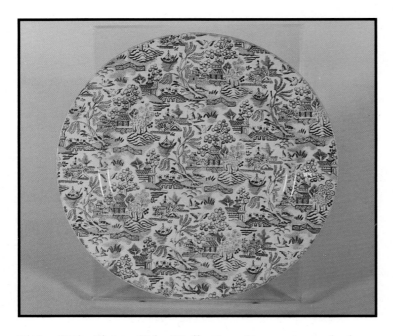

Plate 335. Plate, 8"d, "Calico" pattern, unmarked except for pattern name (note that pattern is the same, except for the border, as Adderley's "Daisy" pattern in the following photograph), Pink Willow.

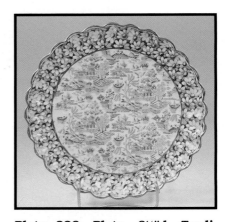

Plate 336. Plate, 8½"d, Traditional patterns cover center, Floral border, "Daisy" pattern name by manufacturer, English, W.A. Adderley mark a.

Plate 337. Plate, 6"d, Mandarin center pattern, Dagger border, English, Samuel Radford, Pink Willow.

Plate 338. Plate, 9"d, reticulated edge, embossed shell designs, Mandarin center pattern, cobalt blue outer border, English, Empire Porcelain Co., see Godden Mark 1499, ca. mid 1900s, Flow Blue Willow.

Plate 339. Plate, 9¼"d, Traditional center and border patterns, English, Charles Meigh & Son (M & S Hanley), Black Willow.

Plate 340. Plate, 9½"d, scalloped edge, Traditional center and border patterns, American, Buffalo Pottery mark a for 1907.

Plate 341. Plate, 9"d, stoneware, ten-sided panelled edge, Traditional center and border patterns, English, unmarked, Mulberry Willow.

Plate 342. Plate, 9"d, scalloped edge, Traditional center and border patterns, English, Allerton mark c, Gaudy Willow (brown underglaze with orange overglaze).

Plate 343. Plate, 7"d, Traditional center and border patterns, unidentified mark, Gaudy Willow (green underglaze, orange overglaze).

Plate 344. Plate, 6"d, Traditional center and border patterns, Japan mark e (Two Phoenix, N.K. Porcelain Co.) Gaudy Willow (multi-colored over and under the glaze).

Plate 345. Plate, 9½"d, Traditional center pattern, cobalt blue outer border, English, attributed to Pinder, Bourne, & Co., ca. 1879 (Godden, June 1987).

Plate 346. Plate, 7¼"d, reticulated edge, Traditional center pattern, English, unmarked.

Plate 347. Plate, 10"d, Two Temples I center pattern, Butterfly border, unmarked c. early 19th century.

Plate 348. Plate, 8½"d, Two Temples II center pattern, Butterfly border, gold trim outer edge, gold dots on inner border, English, G.L. Ashworth impressed mark, see Godden Mark 137.

Plate 349. Plate, 6½"sq, napkin fold edge, Two Temples II center pattern, Butterfly border, gold trim, English, Sampson Bridgwood & Son.

Plate 350. Plate, 11"d, Turner center pattern, Scroll and Flower border, American, company unidentified, marked "Ideal."

Plate 351. Plate, 8"d, Two Temples II, Reversed, Simplified center pattern, American, unmarked, attributed to Southern Potteries' Blue Ridge Line, Trellis shape.

Plate 352. Plate, 8¾"d, Two Temples II, Reversed, simplified center pattern, Floral border (Bridal Gold 1), American, unmarked.

Plate 353. Plate, 7"d, no center pattern, Pictorial border pattern, English, Allerton mark d with "Pavilion."

Plate 354. Plate, 7"d, Variant center pattern, Pictorial border, American, Hopewell China Co. (Ship mark), Hopewell, Virginia, ca. 1920s-1930s (see Lehner, p. 212.)

Plate 355. Plate, 8¾"d, Polychrome Variant pattern, (black underglaze, orange overglaze), English, Mason's mark a, Gaudy Willow. (Note that the center pattern is identical to the one in the following photograph.)

Plate 356. Plate, 9"d, Polychrome Variant pattern (black underglaze; different colors including heavy black, overglaze), English, G.L. Ashworth impressed mark, see Godden Mark 137, Gaudy Willow.

Plate 357. Plate, 10½"d, Polychrome Variant pattern, English, G.L. Ashworth mark a (without England).

Plate 358. Plate, 6"d, Variant center pattern, Pictorial border, unmarked.

Plate 359. Plate, Grill, 10¾"d, Booths center pattern, Bow Knot border, English, Booths mark b.

Plate 360. Plate, Grill, 10¾"d, Traditional motifs, German, illegible mark.

Plate 362. Plate, Grill, 10½"d, Traditional center and border patterns, marked "Made in Japan."

20 to 25 ea

Plate 361. Plate, Grill, Traditional center and border patterns, Made in Japan mark d (Moriyama).

Plate 363. Plate, Grill, 9½"d, Two Temples II, Reversed, center pattern, Traditional border, American, McNichol China.

Plate 365. Plate, Grill, 11"d, Two Temples II, Reversed, Simplified center pattern, Floral border (Bridal Gold #1), American, marked "Made in USA."

Plate 364. Plate, Grill, 10"d, Turner center pattern, Scroll and Flower border, American, Shenango China mark a.

Plate 366. Plate, Hot Water, 9½" x 8¼", Booths center pattern, Bow Knot border, English, Booths mark a. (Hot water is held in bowl space beneath plate; cork on side serves as a stopper for opening.)

Plate 367. Plate, Hot Water, 11"d, Traditional center and border patterns, exterior decoration, English, Unidentified English mark d.

Plate 368. Plate, Snack Set, Plate, 9"d with raised ridge for holding cup, Traditional center and border patterns, marked "Japan."

Plate 370. Plate, Soup, 10"d, Pictorial border pattern, Doulton's "Willow & Aster" pattern, English, Doulton, see Godden mark 1329, Brown Willow.

Plate 369. Plate, Soup, 8½"d, Traditional center pattern, Variant border pattern, brown inner border, gold trim, English, Alfred Meakin Urn mark, similar to Meakin mark a.

Plate 371. Plate, Soup, 9"d, Traditional center and border patterns, American, Shenango China mark a.

Plate 372. Plate, Square shape, 6½"sq, for tea or dessert, Traditional center and border patterns, gold trim, English, H.M. Williamson & Sons (Heathcote China).

Plate 373. Plate, Square shape, 9½"sq, Traditional center and border patterns, English, Arthur J. Wilkinson, see Godden Mark 4176, Multi-colored Willow.

Plate 374. Platter, 7" x 10", Canton pattern, American, marked "Greenwood China" (Trenton, New Jersey).

Plate 375. Platter, 13"l, deep well on one end, two-part scalloped foot (not shown) on opposite end, Traditional center pattern, Dagger border, English, impressed Copeland mark, see Godden Mark 1068, ca. mid 1800s.

Plate 376. Platter, 12¾" x 9½", Traditional center and border patterns, marked "Made in Occupied Japan."

45⁰⁰ to 55⁰⁰

Plate 377. Platter, 14½" x 11", Traditional center and border patterns, English, Johnson Bros., Red Willow.

Plate 378. Platter, 8¾" x 11", rectangular shape with scalloped edge, Traditional center and border patterns, English, John Steventon & Sons mark b, Green Willow.

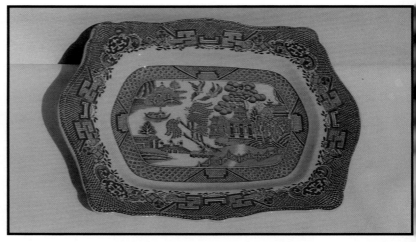

Plate 379. Platter, 9" x 12", Two Temples II, Reversed, Simplified center pattern, Floral border (Bridal Gold #2), American, unmarked.

Plate 380. Platter, 14" x 11¼", Traditional center and border patterns, English, William & Samuel Edge.

225 to 250

Plate 381. Platter, 11¾"l, scalloped edge, Traditional center and border patterns, American, Buffalo Pottery mark a for 1906.

Plate 382. Platter, 10" x 7", Two Temples II center pattern, Butterfly border, marked "Made in Japan."

Plate 383. Platter, Pictorial border, American, marked "National China Co." (see Lehner p. 311).

Plate 384. Platter, 13" x 17", Traditional Simplified center pattern, Pictorial border, American, Sebring Pottery Co. mark a, Multi-colored Willow.

Plate 385. Pudding Mold, 3"h, 4½"d, Two Temples II Simplified center, Pictorial border, English, unmarked, Multi-colored Willow.

Plate 386. Pudding Mold, 4½"h, "England" incised mark.

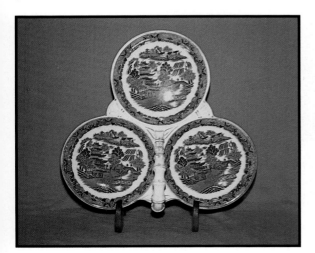

Plate 387, above left: Relish, 4½"sq, nickel silver holder, marked "Beresford EPNS," English, dish made by Doulton, mark b.

Plate 388, above right: Relish, 4⅜"d, Two Temples II Simplified center pattern, Pictorial border, oak holder with metal trim and bail, English, unmarked.

Plate 389, left: Relish, 13"l, three sections with handle (this type of dish is also called a "Caberet"), Two Temples II center pattern, Butterfly border, gold trim, unmarked.

Plate 390. Relish, 11"l, three sections, Mandarin center pattern, Dagger border, English, W.T. Copeland, see Godden Mark 1079.

Plate 391. Relish, 8"l, two sections, lug style handle, English, W.A. Adderley, similar to mark b without "Old Willow."

Plate 392. Relish, 5½"d, scalloped edge, undecorated handle, English, unmarked.

Plate 393. Relish, 8¾"l, scalloped edge, ribbed surface, unmarked.

Plate 394. Relish, 9¼"l, English, W. Adams, marked "W.A. & Co., England," see Godden Mark 27, ca. early 1900s.

Plate 395. Relish, 9½"d, five sections, American, Shenango China mark b.

Plate 396. Relish, 9"l, Booths center pattern, Bow Knot border, English, Wood & Sons mark d.

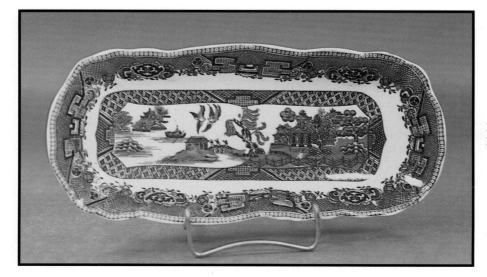

Plate 397. Relish, 11"l, scalloped edge, English, John Maddock.

Plate 398. Relish, 12½"l with 6 matching 6" octagonal shaped plates (these are often called celery or ice cream sets), Traditional center pattern, Variant border pattern, English, Alfred Meakin mark a with "Manchu" as pattern name.

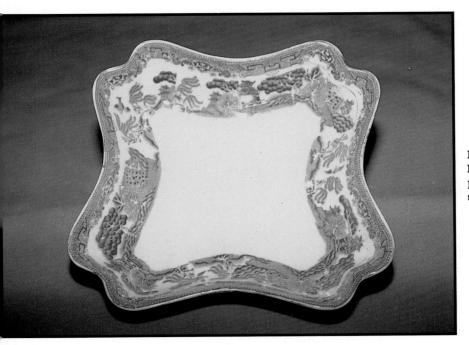

Plate 399. Relish, 9½"sq, widely scalloped edge, Pictorial Border, Traditional pattern, English, A.B. Jones & Sons, see Godden Mark 2199, ca. mid 1900s.

Plate 400. Salt Boxes, 5" x 5", wooden lids, Japanese.

Plate 401. Salt Dip, master, pedestal base, 2"h, 3"d, Traditional border pattern only on exterior, English, unmarked.

Plate 402. Salt Dip, master, pedestal base, 2"h, 3"d, Traditional center and border patterns, English, unmarked.

Plate 403, left: Salt Shaker, 2"h, triangle shape, Japanese.

Plate 404, below: Salt & Pepper Shakers, 3½"h to 4"h, Japanese.

Plate 405. Salt & Pepper Shakers, assorted shapes and sizes, Japanese.

Plate 406. Salt & Pepper Shakers with handles, American, Royal China Co., unmarked, Pink Willow.

Plate 407. Salt & Pepper Shakers, 6"h, wood and ceramic, unmarked.

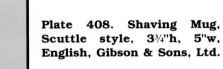

Plate 408. Shaving Mug, Scuttle style, 3¾"h, 5"w, English, Gibson & Sons, Ltd.

Plate 409. Shaving Mug, 3½"h, American, Buffalo Pottery mark a for 1911.

Plate 410. Sherbet Dish or Punch Cup, 3½"h, 3¾"d, Two Temples II center pattern, Butterfly border, marked "Made in Japan."

Plate 411, left: Sherbet Dish or Punch Cup, 3½"h, 3¾"d, Two Temples II reversed center pattern, interior Butterfly border, English, C.T. Maling mark c.

Plate 412, below: Snack Hound, 5 sections, marked "Japan."

Plate 413, left: Soap Pad Holder, 6½"h, marked "Japan."

Plate 414, above, Spice Set, individual "book" style shakers, Japanese.

Plate 415. Spice Set, individual cannisters, 3½"h, tin, Green Willow with blue tops and holder, Mexican (note Spanish names for spices).

Plate 416. Spoon Rack, 9½"l, "Rolling Pin" style, open planter pocket at top, unmarked, Japanese.

Plate 417. Spoon Rack, 8"l, open planter pocket on right side, unmarked, Japanese.

Plate 418. Spoon Rest, double
style, 9"l, Japanese.

Plate 419. Sugar Bowl, open style, footed silver
holder with bail, Mandarin center pattern, Dagger border, English, W.T. Copeland mark b.

Plate 420, above left: Sugar Bowl, 6"h, rope and anchor
finial, unmarked.

Plate 421, above right: Sugar Bowl, 4½"h, white glass,
Traditional Simplified center pattern, Line border, American, unmarked, attributed to Hazel Atlas Glass Company, Red Willow.

Plate 422, left: Sugar Bowl, 3½"h, marked "Japan."

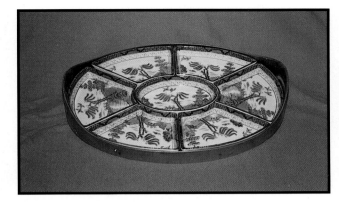

Plate 423. Supper Tray, 16½"l, 11½"w, seven sectional dishes, Booths center pattern, Bow Knot border, English, Booths mark a without "Willow."

Plate 424. Supper Tray, 13" x 11", porcelain, three sectional diamond shaped dishes in six-sided wooden tray, English, "Spode" impressed, early 19th century.

Plate 425. Syrup Pitcher (lid is missing), 6"h, English, Doulton mark b, Flow Blue Willow.

Plate 426. Syrup Pitcher (lid is missing), 6½"h, Two Temples II reversed center pattern, Butterfly border, English, Wedgwood & Co. mark c, Flow Blue Willow.

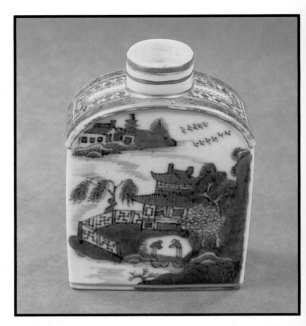

Plate 427. Tea Caddy, 5"h (stopper missing), Variant pattern, gold trim, English, 19th century, unmarked.

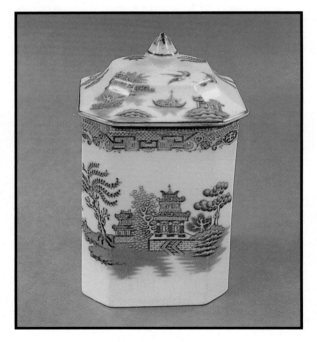

Plate 428, above left: Tea Jar, 7½"h, eight sided, English, Gibson & Sons (with "Jappa" as pattern name).

Plate 429, above right: Tea Jar, 8"h, Two Temples II body pattern, Butterfly border, English, marked "Ringtons Limited, Tea Merchants, Newcastle upon Tyne."

Plate 430, left: Tea Cannister, 10½" h, tin, combination of Two Temples II and Traditional patterns, Scotland, marked "John Buchanan & Bros., Limited, Stewart St. Cowcaddens, Glasgow, Makers of Confections & Chocolates."

Plate 431. Tea Cannisters, 5½"h, chrome, plastic finials, unmarked; a Preserve Jar (not shown) matches these tins.

Plate 432. Tea (Cosy) Pots: left, 5"h, English, made by Wood & Sons for Abram Allware, Ltd., trade mark "Cosy"; right; 7"h, English, unmarked.

Plate 433. Tea (Cosy) Pot (a stacked teapot, sugar, and creamer set is also called a "Cosy Pot"), two-cup capacity, marked "Japan."

Plate 434. Tea (Cosy) Pot, 2-cup capacity, marked "Japan." 120⁰⁰ to 140⁰⁰

157

Plate 435. Teapot, 5"h, 10" spout to handle, and Trivet, 7½"d, Burleigh center patterns and Butterfly borders, English, Burgess & Leigh mark c (Burleigh Ware).

Plate 436. Teapot, 6"h, Canton pattern, English, G.L. Ashworth mark b.

Plate 437. Teapot, Mandarin pattern on body, Variant border, English, C.T. Maling mark a.

Plate 438. Teapot, with matching Sugar Bowl and Creamer, English, Allerton mark d.

Plate 439. Teapot, Worcester center pattern, Scroll and Flower border, porcelain, gold trim, English, Worcester mark a for 1886.

Plate 440. Teapot, musical type, Japanese, unmarked.

Plate 441. Teapot, 4"h, 8" spout to handle, English, Mintons, see Godden Mark 2713 (with England added), ca. early 1900s.

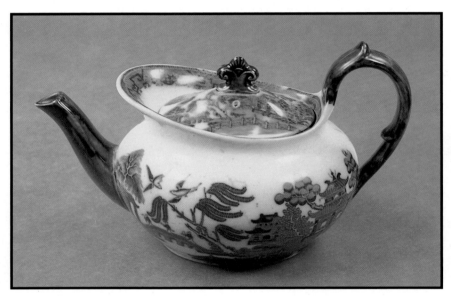

Plate 442. Teapot, 4"h, 7½" spout to handle, English, Doulton mark a.

Plate 443. Teapot, 4"h, short opening rather than true spout, Traditional pattern on body, Dagger border pattern, English, marked "The Hexagon, Sadler, Burslem, England," similar to Godden's Mark 3346 (impressed).

Plate 444. Teapot, 6"h, individual two-cup size, gold ring shaped finial, gold trim, Traditional body pattern, Borderless except for design of crosses on handle, English, James Sadler & Sons.

Plate 445. Teapots: Left, 5¾"h; right, 4¾"h, fancy finial, "cane" style spouts and handles, English, Ridgways mark a.

Plate 446. Teapot, 4-cup capacity, English, marked "North Staffordshire Pottery Co., Ltd," see Godden p. 469, ca. 1940s.

Plate 447. Teapot, 6-cup capacity, American, unmarked, Homer Laughlin.

Plate 448. Teapot, 6-cup capacity, American, unmarked, Royal China Company.

Plate 449. Teapot, 6-cup capacity, English, Johnson Bros., Red Willow.

Plate 450. Teapot, 8"h, Pictorial Border, Traditional pattern, English, Myott, Son & Co.

Plate 451. Teapot, 3½"h, 2-cup capacity, Two Temples II pattern on body, Butterfly border, C.T. Maling mark b without "Made in England."

Plate 452. Teapot, 3¼"h, 2-cup capacity, matching cup and saucer, Two Temples II pattern on body, Butterfly border, unmarked.

Plate 453. Teapot, 6-cup capacity, matching trivet, Two Temples II pattern on body, Butterfly border, English, Keeling & Co., see Godden Mark 2243.

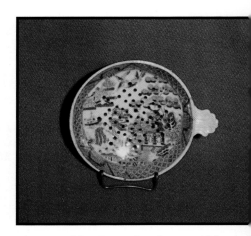

Plate 454. Tea Set: Teapot, Sugar Creamer, Coffee Cup and Tea Cup, porcelain, Traditional pattern with "Auld Lang Syne" verse printed on borders, lion finials and trim painted gold, English, W.T. Copeland, see Godden Mark 1077 (with for "Tiffany & Co., New York").

Plate 455. Tea Strainer, 4"d, unmarked.

Plate 456, above left: Tea Tile, 5⅝"sq, English, impressed mark "Minton's China Works," Black and Gray Willow.

Plate 457, above right: Tea Tile, 7¼"sq., woven cane border, Japanese, unmarked.

Plate 458, left: Tea Tile, 8"d, in 2" wooden frame unmarked.

Plate 459. Tea Waste Bowl, 3"h, 6"d, unmarked, English.

Plate 460. Tea Waste Bowl, 3½"h, 6½"d, English, Doulton mark b, Flow Blue Willow.

Plate 462. Toast Cover or Warmer, 3½"h, 6"d, American, The Bailey Walker Co.

Plate 461. Temple Jar, 8"h, marked "Made in England."

Plate 463. Toaster, 7"h, 7"w, American, Pan Electrical Mfg. Co., Cleveland, Ohio, Two Temples II, Reversed, and Traditional patterns combined.

Plate 464. Toast Rack, 6"l, English Grimwades, see Godden Mark 1832.

Plate 465, left: Toby Pitchers, 5½"h, English left, William Kent; right, unmarked.

Plate 466, above: Toothpick Holder, 2¼"h, American, Buffalo China.

Plate 467, above: Toothpick Holder, 2¼"h, Traditional pattern, Variant border, English, Josiah Wedgwood mark b.

Plate 468, right: Tray, 19"d, Reversed Traditional pattern, unmarked, ca. 1950s.

Plate 469. Tray, 16"l, papier mâché, Traditional center pattern, Variant border, marked "Made in Occupied Japan, Alcohol Proof," Multi-colored Willow.

Plate 470. Tray, 11½"d, silver plated.

Plate 471, above left: Tray, 16"d, brass, English, unmarked.

Plate 472, above right: Trivet, wrought iron frame, Japanese.

Plate 473, right: Trivet, 5½"d, unmarked, English.

Plate 474. Vases, pair, 4¾"h, silver rims, English, marked "British Made" with crossed swords emblem and initials "R, P, and S," (unidentified company).

Plate 475. Vases, pair, 5¼"h, English, Doulton mark b with "Made in England."

Plate 476. Vase, 7"h, pillow or canteen shape, English, "Mintons" impressed mark, year cypher for 1873, see Godden Mark 2711 and p. 440.

Plate 477. Vase, 7½"h, cylinder shape, footed, English, "Mintons" impressed mark, year cypher for 1875, see Godden Mark 2711 and p. 440, Flow Blue Willow.

Plate 478. Vase, 6"h, stoneware, English, Doulton, see Godden Mark 1344.

Plate 479. Vase, 12"h, English, Josiah Wedgwood mark b (without Etruria, England).

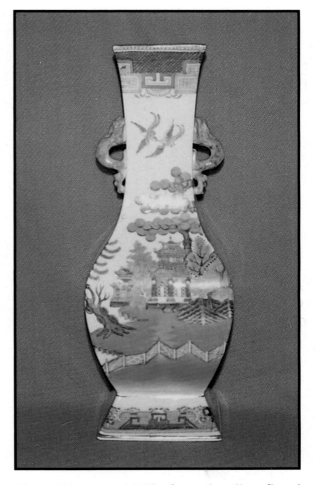

Plate 480. Vase, 14¼"h, fancy handles, flared base, unmarked, Multi-colored Willow.

Plate 481. Vase, 9"h, ovoid shape, ring-style handles, English, Cauldon, see Godden Mark 821, Multi-colored Willow.

Plate 482. Wall Plaque, 7"d, brass plate in 2¼"w oak frame, English.

Plate 483. Wall Plaque, 9"d, plate in 4½"w aluminum surround, American, Homer Laughlin mark c for 1945.

Plate 484, Wall Pocket, 6"h, Simplified Traditional pattern on body, Floral border, Japanese.

Plate 485, left: Wash Set: Bowl & Pitcher, English, Doulton mark b, Flow Blue Willow. (The following items match this set.)

Plate 486, below: Soap Dish and Drainer, 5½"d, English, Doulton mark d with "Made in England."

Plate 488. Chamber Pot, 5½"h, 9¼"d, English, Doulton mark b.

Plate 487. Toothbrush Holder, 5"h, English, Doulton mark d with "Made in England."

Plate 489. Wash Set: Bowl & Pitcher, Two Temples II pattern, Butterfly border, English, marked "Semi-China" in a square and "B.T. & S.E.B." and Crown impressed, unidentified company.

Plate 490. Wash Set: Bowl & Pitcher, Toothbrush Holder, Covered Soap Dish and Drainer, English, C.T. Maling & Sons mark b without "Made in England."

Plate 491. Wash Set: Bowl & Pitcher, English, Josiah Wedgwood mark b with impressed "Wedgwood."

Plate 492. Chamber Pot matching Wedgwood Bowl and Pitcher in preceding photograph.

Plate 493, above: Wash Set: Bowl & Pitcher, English, John Tams, Ltd (Tams Ware), Multi-colored Willow.

Plate 494, right: Chamber Pot, 9¾"h (excluding lid), Traditional center pattern, Floral border pattern, English, unmarked, Green Willow.

The following photographs were not "alphabetized" into the book because it seemed more appropriate to show the various items as "groups" rather than singly. A few examples of the Burleigh pattern are included in the first part of the book, but a variety of modern pieces are shown together here. Most of these are from Lynda Galloway's collection and were ordered from Cashs' Catalog in Ireland around 1985. Some are not currently being offered for sale. Prices shown are retail for 1985-1987 and are, of course, subject to change.

Blue Willow ware made in England, Japan, and Taiwan which is distributed by Heritage Mint, Ltd. in Scottsdale, Arizona, is included in this section. The English pieces carry the "Churchill," mark, or "Blue Willow Pantry Collections" or "Broadhurst Staffordshire, Made in England," a new backstamp issued in 1987. Prices are for 1987 and are subject to change. Heritage Marketing should be contacted for current price information.

Examples of paper items such as plates, cups, napkins, and greeting cards are from Marcie Williams' collection. Linens and pages from some old magazines featuring the Blue Willow pattern are from Rachel and Jim Lafferty's collection. Prices are not quoted for the paper and linen items.

An example of "quilling" (rolling very thin strips of colored paper together to form a particular pattern which is glued onto a backing) was made by Angelina Tagliaferri. The last photograph is of a print made from the original oil and water color painting by South Carolina artist, Ravenel Gaillard.

Plate 495, above: Ewer, 9"h and Basin, 19"d. (This and the following 5 photographs are modern examples of the Burleigh pattern with the Scroll and Flower border, English, Burgess and Leigh.)

Plate 496, right: Coffee Pot, 8¼"h, 5-cup capacity.

Plate 497. Salt & Pepper, 4¾"h; Gravy Boat, 8-oz. capacity.

Plate 498. Candle Sticks, 6"h.

Plate 499. Tiered Serving Dish, 10"d (lower plate); 4¾"d (small plates).

Plate 500. Set of Platters:
15½" x 12"; 13¼" x 10¼";
10" x 7½".

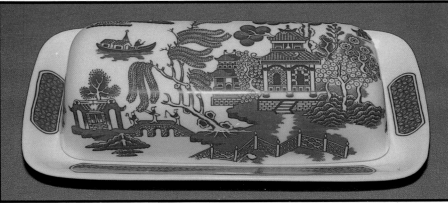

Plate 501. Butter Dish, ¼ lb. This and the following 2 photographs are offered by Heritage Marketing International. They carry the "Churchill" mark.

Plate 502. Coffee Pot, 9"h.

Plate 503. Covered Casserole, 9"d.

Plate 504. Mixing Bowl Set with plastic covers, unmarked. (Heritage Marketing).

Plate 505. Casserole Dishes: 7"l Baker and 13"l au gratin Dish, part of the Blue Willow Pantry Collection made in Japan for Heritage Mint, Ltd.

Plate 506. Cookware Set, 7 pieces, part of the Blue Willow Pantry Collection made in Taiwan for Heritage Mint, Ltd.

Plate 507. Tea Kettle, part of the Blue Willow Pantry Collection, made in Taiwan for Heritage Mint, Ltd.

Plate 508. Change of Address Card and Gift Tag in the shape of a cup.

Plate 509. Two styles of Note Cards.

Plate 510. Paper Plate, Hot Cup, Cold Cup.

Plate 511. Three types of Napkins and wax Candles.

Plate 512. Plastic Plate, 9½"d, Traditional pattern reversed, unmarked.

Plate 513. Plastic Plate, 10"d, Traditional pattern with extra birds, American, made by Melmac.

Plate 514. Blue Willow Decal.

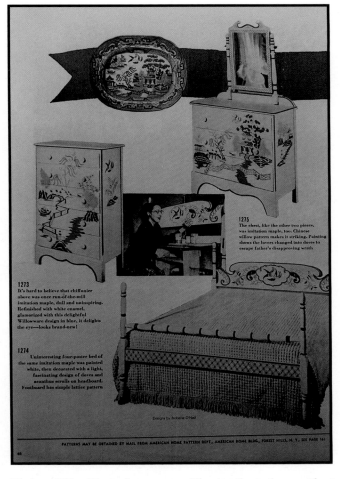

Plate 515. Magazine page illustrating decorating with the Blue Willow pattern.

Plate 516. Magazine page illustrating Blue Willow table cloth and napkins as well as plates on the wall.

Plate 517. Roll Basket lined with Blue Willow patterned material.

Plate 518. Linen Place Mat with part of Blue Willow scene.

Plate 519. Blue Willow Traditional center pattern made by "quilling" (Angelina Tagliaferri).

Plate 520. "Mixed Bouquet" print of painting featuring a Blue Willow planter and background (Ravenel Gaillard).

Glossary

Bisque - unglazed porcelain.

Body - the clay composition of an article.

Bone China - a ceramic class made from calcined animal bone ash (at least 50% of the paste mixture) with china clay and feldspar composing the rest. Josiah Spode I invented this form in the late 1700's. England is the primary producer of bone china which is translucent and considered a form of porcelain.

Bow Knot - a border characteristic found on Blue Willow patterns.

China - a term appropriate only to hard paste porcelain; frequently used for any ceramic.

Cobalt - ore found in copper, silver and tin mines. The oxide formed from this mineral produces a substance (cobalt blue) used for coloring ceramics.

Crazing - fine lines appearing on the glaze of earthenwares caused by heat or age.

Earthenware - pottery having a porosity of more than 5%. It is made from many different types of natural clays including kaolin, ball clay, and cornish stone. Earthenwares are opaque and may be glazed or unglazed.

Fishroe - a term referring to the outer border characteristic of several Blue Willow border patterns composed of a series of squares or circles with dots in the middle.

Glaze - a liquid applied to ceramic bodies for decoration and/or to achieve vitreosity.

Hard Paste - a class of ceramics whose primary ingredient is kaolin, a type of earth containing hydrated aluminum silicates. Kaolin accounts for 50% of the paste with feldspar being the other main ingredient. It is called "hard" paste porcelain because it is fired at extremely high temperatures. Hard paste is also referred to as true or natural porcelain since its chief components exist naturally in the earth. Hard paste porcelain is translucent and vitreous if glazed. It is very strong and does not craze.

Impressed - marks that are made in the form of a stamp and pressed into the body of a ceramic body before it is fired.

Incised - marks that are sharply cut into the clay body of an object before it is fired.

Ironstone - a type of stoneware patented by Mason in England in 1813. Iron slag is pulverized and mixed with the clay to form this type of ceramic body.

Monochrome - one color decoration.

Nankin - inner border on willow pattern ceramics.

Opaque - meaning that light cannot pass through an object.

Overglaze - refers to handpainted or transfer decoration applied to a ceramic object after a glaze has been applied and fired on. It shows wear through time and can be damaged.

Paste - the clay mixture used to form the body of ceramic objects.

Polychrome - the use of more than one color in decorating ceramic items.

Porcelain - ceramics that are translucent and usually vitreous. The term usually refers to true or hard paste porcelain.

Pottery - any object made of clay and fired at a high temperature.

Printed Marks - simple handpainted initials or marks, either initial forms or more elaborate, made in the form of a stamp or transfer applied to a ceramic body over or under glaze.

Semi-Porcelain - earthenware ceramics. Semi-porcelain objects are opaque and non-vitreous.

Spur Marks- small rough spots made by the clay supports which hold and separate ceramic plates and platters in the kiln during the firing process.

Staffordshire Knot - a printed mark in the form of a bow used by many Staffordshire potters during the 19th century.

Stoneware - pottery with a porosity of less than 5%. It is glazed and fired only once, at extremely high temperatures, until it is vitrified. Stoneware is made from natural clays of a sedimentary type, fine grained and plastic. It is opaque, heavy and quite durable.

Transfer - a method of decorating ceramics where a design is engraved on a copper plate. The lines of the design are filled with paint and the plate is placed on a hot copper plate. A tissue paper, covered with a soapy mixture, is first pressed into the engraved design, then placed to an object face down (transferred) and rubbed hard onto the object. The object is coated with a varnish and is also heated so that the pattern will stick. When the piece is dry, the paper is washed off.

Translucent - allowing light to pass through. This term refers to the chief characteristic of porcelain.

Underglaze - handpainted or transfer patterns or decorations applied to the body of a ceramic object before a glaze is applied which is permanent and cannot be destroyed.

Vitreous - meaning glass-like. This state is achieved on ceramic bodies by glazes made of glass-forming materials that are applied to the ceramic body and fired at a high temperature until the object and glaze fuse together becoming one entity.

Bibliography

Altman, Seymour and Violet. *The Book of Buffalo Pottery.* New York: Bonanza Books, 1969.

Andacht, Sandra, Nancy Garthe, and Robert Mascarelli. *Wallace-Homestead Price Guide to Oriental Antiques.* Des Moines, IA: Wallace-Homestead Book Company, 1981.

Barber, Edwin Atlee. *Marks of American Potters.* First published in 1904, reprinted in 1976 by Feingold and Lewis, New York.

____. *The Ceramic Collector's Glossary.* First published in 1914, reprinted in 1967 by Da Capo Press, New York.

Biernacki, Conrad. "As Yet Uncharted Boundaries: The Willow Borders," *The Willow Notebook,* January 1981.

____. "The Butterfly Border," *The Willow Notebook,* November, 1981.

____. "Willow Pattern China," *National Journal,* April, 1982.

Biernacki, Conrad (ed.). *The Willow Transfer Quarterly,* January, April, July, 1983; January, 1984.

Biernacki, Conrad and Connie Rogers. "More on Borders: A Full House Now," *The Willow Notebook,* May, 1981.

____. "Willow Centre Patterns," *The Willow Notebook,* September, 1981.

____. "Willow Centre Patterns (addendum)," *The Willow Notebook,* September, 1982.

Blue Willow Inc., Catalog, 1987, Buffalo, New York.

Boger, Louise Ade. *The Dictionary of World Pottery and Porcelain.* New York: Charles Scribner's Sons, 1971.

Burgess, A.M. *History of the Willow Pattern.* Published privately, 1904.

Cashs' of Ireland, Catalog, 1985, 1986, 1987.

Copeland, Robert. *Spode's Willow Pattern and Other Designs after the Chinese.* New York: Rizzoli, 1980.

Coysh, A.H. *Blue and White Transfer Ware 1780-1840.* Rutland, VT: Charles E. Tuttle Company, 1971.

Gaston, Mary Frank. *The Collector's Encyclopedia of Limoges Porcelain.* Paducah, KY: Collector Books, 1980.

____. *Blue Willow.* Paducah, KY: Collector Books, 1983; 1986 (revised).

Godden, Geoffrey A. *Victorian Porcelain.* New York: Thomas Nelson & Sons, 1961.

____. *British Pottery and Porcelain, 1780-1850.* New York: A.S. Barnes and Co., Inc., 1963.

____. *Encyclopedia of British Pottery and Porcelain Marks.* New York: Crown Publishers, 1964.

____. *Handbook of British Pottery & Porcelain Marks.* New York: Frederick A. Praeger, 1968.

____. *Godden's Guide to English Porcelain.* London: Hart-Davis, MacGibbon, Granada Publishing, 1978.

____. *Oriental Export Market Porcelain.* London: Granada, 1979.

____. Correspondence to Lynda Lehmann-Galloway, June 23, 1987.

____. Correspondence to Lynda Lehmann-Galloway, September 14, 1987.

Hughes, G. Bernard. *The Collector's Pocket Book of China.* New York: Award Books; London: Tandem Books, 1965.

Huxford, Sharon and Box Huxford. *Schroeder's Antiques Price Guide.* Paducah, KY: Collector Books, 1988; 1989.

Jenkins, Dorothy A. *The Woman's Day Book of Antiques and Collectibles.* Patterson, N.J; The Main Street Press William Case House, 1981.

Kovel, Ralph M. and Terry H. Kovel. *Dictionary of Marks, Pottery and Porcelain.* New York: Crown Publishers, Inc., 1953.

Lehner, Lois. *Ohio Pottery and Glass, Marks and Manufacturers.* Des Moines, IA: Wallace-Homestead, 1978.

____. *Lehner's Encyclopedia of U.S. Marks on Pottery, Porcelain & Clay.* Paducah, KY: Collector Books, 1988.

Little, W.A. *Staffordshire Blue.* London: B.T. Batsford, Ltd., 1969.

Misiewicz, Lois (ed.). *The Willow Notebook,* Number 11-34, January 1980-November 1983.

Loehr, Louise M. *Collector's Price Guide to Willow Pattern China.* Kutztown, Pa: Louise's Old Things, 1987.

Mountfield, David (comp.). *The Antique Collector's Illustrated Dictionary.* New York: Hamlyn, 1974.

Murphy, Catherine and Kyle Husfloen (eds.). *The Antique Trader Antiques and Collectibles Price Guide.* Dubuque, Ia: The Babka Publishing Co., 1987.

Poche, Emanuel. *Porcelain Marks of the World.* New York: Arco Publishing Co., Inc., 1974.

Rogers, Connie. "Willow Ware from Ohio," *National Journal,* August, 1981.

____. "Blue Willow Plates," *Depression Glass Daze,* September, 1981.

____. "More Blue Willow Grill Plates," *Depression Glass Daze,* August, 1982.

____. "American Willow Variant Patterns, Part I—Decals Over-Glaze," *The Daze,* September, 1987.

____. "American Willow Variants, Part I—Transfer-printed Wares," *The "New" Glaze,* May-June, 1987.

____. "American Willow Variants, Part II—Institutional Ware (4 parts)," *The "New" Glaze,* July—October, 1987.

____. "American Willow Variant Patterns III—Decals Over-Glaze," *The "New" Glaze,* November, 1987-March, 1988.

____. "The Shenango China Co.," *The "New" Glaze,* April, 1988.

____. "American Willow Variants, Part IV—Rubber Stamp Patterns," *The "New" Glaze,* May-July, 1988.

Rogers, Connie (ed.). *Ohio Willow Society Newsletter,* July, September, November, 1986: January, March, May, July, 1987.

____. *American Willow Report* (bi-monthly newsletter), September, 1987-July, 1988.

Rogers, Connie and Conrad Biernacki. "Willow Borders Illustrated I and II," *The Willow Notebook,* July 1981.

Sandon, Henry. *Royal Worcester Porcelain from 1862 to the Present Day.* London: Barrie & Jenkins, 1973.

Spinning Wheel, April, 1968.

Van Patten, Joan F. *The Collector's Encyclopedia of Nippon Porcelain.* Paducah, KY: Collector Books, 1979.

Worth, Veryl Marie. *Willow Pattern China.* Revised 2nd edition. H.S. Worth Co., 1979. Distributed by Fact Book Company, Oakridge, OR.

____. *Collectors Price Guide to Willow Pattern China,* 1981. Distributed by Fact Book Company, Oakridge, OR.

Worth, Veryl Marie and Louise M. Loehr. *Willow Pattern China.* Revised 3rd edition. H.S. Worth Co., 1986. Distributed by Louise's Old Things, Kutztown, Pa.

Index to Objects

(All numbers refer to Plate Numbers)

Index to Willow Patterns

Willow center patterns with their border patterns are indexed by photograph number. Pieces with the Traditional center and border pattern or partial versions of the Traditional patterns are not indexed because they compose the majority of the examples illustrated. Pieces decorated with only the Traditional border pattern and examples of the Traditional center pattern with a border different from the Traditional border are indexed. The patterns are listed alphabetically.

Index to English Manufacturers

Index to Japanese Items

Index to American Manufacturers

Index to Origin other than England, Japan, United States

Price Guide

Plate 1......................$35.00–45.00
Plate 2......................$25.00–30.00
Plate 3......................$40.00–45.00
Plate 4...............ea. $45.00–55.00
Plate 5......................$30.00–35.00
Plate 6......................$25.00–30.00
Plate 7...............ea. $250.00–275.00
Plate 8......................$50.00–60.00
Plate 9...............set $150.00–175.00
Plate 10.............set $250.00–300.00
Plate 11....................$175.00–200.00
Plate 12....................$150.00–175.00
Plate 13....................$150.00–175.00
Plate 14....................$225.00–250.00
Plate 15....................$225.00–250.00
Plate 16....................$45.00–55.00
Plate 17....................$45.00–55.00
Plate 18....................$60.00–75.00
Plate 19............set $800.00–1,000.00
Plate 20....................$200.00–225.00
Plate 21....................$800.00–1,000.00
Plate 22....................$375.00–425.00
Plate 23....................$800.00–1,000.00
Plate 24.............set $600.00–800.00
Plate 25....................$275.00–325.00
Plate 26....................$225.00–275.00
Plate 27....................$150.00–175.00
Plate 28....................$130.00–160.00
Plate 29....................$120.00–140.00
Plate 30....................$800.00–1,000.00
Plate 31....................$30.00–35.00
Plate 32....................$80.00–90.00
Plate 33.............set $120.00–140.00
Plate 34.............set $200.00–225.00
Plate 35...............ea. $15.00–20.00
Plate 36. Left:..............$25.00–30.00
            Right:............$35.00–40.00
Plate 37....................$100.00–120.00
Plate 38...............ea. $20.00–25.00
Plate 39. Left:..............$15.00–20.00
            Right:............$12.00–15.00
Plate 40....................$80.00–95.00
Plate 41....................$800.00–1,000.00
Plate 42....................$100.00–120.00
Plate 43....................$70.00–90.00
Plate 44....................$130.00–150.00
Plate 45....................$400.00–500.00
Plate 46. 8" Bowl........$65.00–75.00
            10" Bowl.......$75.00–85.00
Plate 47....................$85.00–95.00
Plate 48....................$220.00–240.00
Plate 49....................$25.00–30.00
Plate 50....................$55.00–65.00
Plate 51....................$25.00–35.00
Plate 52....................$15.00–20.00
Plate 53....................$20.00–25.00
Plate 54....................$70.00–80.00
Plate 55....................$100.00–120.00
Plate 56....................$120.00–135.00
Plate 57....................$275.00–300.00
Plate 58. (lid only).....$150.00–175.00
Plate 59....................$225.00–250.00

Plate 60....................$250.00–275.00
Plate 61....................$150.00–175.00
Plate 62....................$250.00–275.00
Plate 63....................$250.00–275.00
Plate 64....................$120.00–150.00
Plate 65. (3 pc. set)..$250.00–300.00
Plate 66. (4 pc. set)..$300.00–350.00
Plate 67....................$130.00–150.00
Plate 68....................$160.00–180.00
Plate 69....................$75.00–100.00
Plate 70....................$60.00–75.00
Plate 71....................$120.00–140.00
Plate 72....................$200.00–225.00
Plate 73....................$200.00–225.00
Plate 74....................$55.00–65.00
Plate 75....................$175.00–200.00
Plate 76....................$800.00–1,000.00
Plate 77....................$450.00–550.00
Plate 78....................$600.00–800.00
Plate 79....................$150.00–175.00
Plate 80...............set $225.00–275.00
Plate 81. Tureen......$150.00–175.00
            Ladle.........$140.00–160.00
Plate 82....................$125.00–150.00
Plate 83....................$325.00–375.00
Plate 84....................$200.00–250.00
Plate 85....................$60.00–75.00
Plate 86....................$60.00–75.00
Plate 87....................$80.00–100.00
Plate 88....................$85.00–95.00
Plate 89...............ea. $25.00–35.00
Plate 90...............set $75.00–100.00
Plate 91...............set $225.00–250.00
Plate 92.............pair $250.00–275.00
Plate 93.............pair $400.00–500.00
Plate 94....................$80.00–100.00
Plate 95....................$150.00–175.00
Plate 96...............set $350.00–450.00
Plate 97...............set $100.00–125.00
Plate 98....................$225.00–275.00
Plate 99....................$200.00–225.00
Plate 100..................$200.00–225.00
Plate 101..................$200.00–225.00
Plate 102. Sugar...........$75.00–85.00
            Cup/Saucer ..$70.00–85.00
Plate 103..................$175.00–200.00
Plate 104..................$30.00–40.00
Plate 105. Grill Plate......$50.00–60.00
            Cake Plate.....$50.00–60.00
            Tin Plate........$12.00–15.00
Plate 106. ....set..$400.00–500.00
Plate 107. Plate..........$25.00–30.00
            Gravy/UP.......$90.00–100.00
            Cov. Veg/UP.$120.00–140.00
            Platter..........$70.00–90.00
Plate 108. ....set $175.00–200.00
Plate 109. ....set in box $80.00–100.00
Plate 110. ....set $60.00–70.00
Plate 111. Choc. Pot ...$175.00–200.00
            Cups (ea.).....$30.00–45.00
Plate 112. ....set $450.00–550.00
Plate 113. ....$140.00–160.00

Plate 114. ....$140.00–160.00
Plate 115...................$30.00–35.00
Plate 116...................$30.00–35.00
Plate 117...............ea. $45.00–55.00
Plate 118............set $150.00–175.00
Plate 119...................$60.00–75.00
Plate 120...................$35.00–45.00
Plate 121...................$80.00–100.00
Plate 122...................$100.00–120.00
Plate 123...................$90.00–110.00
Plate 124...................$90.00–110.00
Plate 125. ......set $3,000.00–3,500.00
Plate 126...................$125.00–150.00
Plate 127...................$325.00–375.00
Plate 128...................$400.00–450.00
Plate 129...................$50.00–60.00
Plate 130...................$700.00–800.00
Plate 131...................$200.00–250.00
Plate 132............set $250.00–300.00
Plate 133............set $175.00–200.00
Plate 134........set $1,400.00–1,600.00
Plate 135............set $200.00–225.00
Plate 136............set $275.00–300.00
Plate 137...................$40.00–50.00
Plate 138...................$50.00–65.00
Plate 139............set $250.00–300.00
Plate 140...........$2,200.00–2,500.00
Plate 141...........$1,200.00–1,400.00
Plate 142........ea. $1,200.00–1,400.00
Plate 143...............ea. $20.00–40.00
Plate 144...................$40.00–45.00
Plate 145...................$30.00–35.00
Plate 146...................$30.00–35.00
Plate 147...................$50.00–60.00
Plate 148...................$10.00–15.00
Plate 149...................$8.00–12.00
Plate 150...................$75.00–85.00
Plate 151...................$60.00–75.00
Plate 152. ....set $125.00–150.00
Plate 153. ....set $50.00–60.00
Plate 154. ....set $80.00–90.00
Plate 155. ....set $70.00–80.00
Plate 156...................$35.00–45.00
Plate 157...................$45.00–55.00
Plate 158...............ea. $60.00–75.00
Plate 159...................$12.00–15.00
Plate 160...............ea. $45.00–55.00
Plate 161...................$14.00–18.00
Plate 162...................$40.00–50.00
Plate 163...................$50.00–60.00
Plate 164...................$60.00–70.00
Plate 165...................$45.00–55.00
Plate 166...................$80.00–90.00
Plate 167...................$120.00–130.00
Plate 168...................$65.00–75.00
Plate 169...................$75.00–85.00
Plate 170...Comp. set $175.00–200.00
Plate 171. ....ea. $35.00–40.00
Plate 172...................$10.00–15.00
Plate 173...................$8.00–12.00
Plate 174...................$10.00–15.00
Plate 175. ....ea. $6.00–10.00

Plate 176. ....(mc) $70.00–80.00
Plate 177....................$35.00–40.00
Plate 178..................$150.00–175.00
Plate 179....................$55.00–65.00
Plate 180....................$50.00–60.00
Plate 181....................$70.00–80.00
Plate 182....................$35.00–45.00
Plate 183....................$40.00–45.00
Plate 184....................$35.00–40.00
Plate 185.....................$5.00–10.00
Plate 186....................$20.00–25.00
Plate 187....................$45.00–55.00
Plate 188....................$15.00–18.00
Plate 189....................$35.00–45.00
Plate 190....................$40.00–50.00
Plate 191....................$80.00–90.00
Plate 192. ....set $175.00–200.00
Plate 193....................$30.00–35.00
Plate 194....................$30.00–35.00
Plate 195....................$25.00–30.00
Plate 196....................$20.00–25.00
Plate 197..................$250.00–300.00
Plate 198. Butter.....ea. $50.00–60.00
          Meat........$100.00–120.00
Plate 199..................$350.00–400.00
Plate 200..................$250.00–300.00
Plate 201..................$350.00–400.00
Plate 202. Left $100.00–125.00
          Right $150.00–175.00
Plate 203....................$225.00–250.00
Plate 204. ....ea. $25.00–35.00
Plate 205. ....ea. $100.00–120.00
Plate 206. Left $30.00–40.00
          Middle..........$30.00–40.00
          Right $30.00–40.00
Plate 207. Left Pr........ $50.00–60.00
          Right Pr....... $30.00–40.00
Plate 208. Stand......$300.00–350.00
          Egg Cups..ea. $35.00–45.00
Plate 209..................$550.00–650.00
Plate 210..............$800.00–1,000.00
Plate 211. ....set $300.00–350.00
Plate 212. ....place set $45.00–55.00
Plate 213....................$45.00–55.00
Plate 214....................$45.00–55.00
Plate 215....................$90.00–100.00
Plate 216....................$60.00–70.00
Plate 217....................$35.00–45.00
Plate 218. ....ea. $20.00–25.00
Plate 219. ....ea. $20.00–25.00
Plate 220. Left $16.00–20.00
          Right $12.00–15.00
Plate 221....................$75.00–85.00
Plate 222. Small......ea. $15.00–25.00
          Medium ..ea. $15.00–25.00
          Large ......ea. $15.00–25.00
Plate 223. ....ea. $15.00–20.00
Plate 224. ....ea. $15.00–20.00
Plate 225. Pitcher $120.00–140.00
          Glasses...ea. $35.00–40.00
Plate 226..................$125.00–150.00
Plate 227....................$90.00–110.00
Plate 228....................$70.00–80.00
Plate 229....................$80.00–90.00

Plate 230....................$55.00–65.00
Plate 231....................$75.00–85.00
Plate 232....................$45.00–55.00
Plate 233....................$40.00–45.00
Plate 234....................$55.00–65.00
Plate 235....................$40.00–50.00
Plate 236....................$50.00–60.00
Plate 237..................$300.00–350.00
Plate 238..................$225.00–275.00
Plate 239..................$500.00–600.00
Plate 240..................$250.00–300.00
Plate 241..................$150.00–175.00
Plate 242..................$400.00–500.00
Plate 243....................$12.00–15.00
Plate 244..................$175.00–200.00
Plate 245..................$250.00–275.00
Plate 246..................$325.00–375.00
Plate 247..................$450.00–550.00
Plate 248..................$250.00–300.00
Plate 249..................$110.00–135.00
Plate 250..................$140.00–165.00
Plate 251. 12¼" $175.00–200.00
          7" $140.00–160.00
Plate 252....................$120.00–140.00
Plate 253....................$45.00–55.00
Plate 254. 8" $80.00–100.00
          8½" $100.00–120.00
          11½" $125.00–150.00
Plate 255..................$250.00–300.00
Plate 256..................$350.00–400.00
Plate 257..................$225.00–275.00
Plate 258. Left $130.00–150.00
          Right $160.00–175.00
Plate 259..................$400.00–500.00
Plate 260..................$400.00–500.00
Plate 261....................$30.00–40.00
Plate 262....................$75.00–85.00
Plate 263....................$75.00–85.00
Plate 264....................$90.00–100.00
Plate 265....................$130.00–150.00
Plate 266....................$90.00–100.00
Plate 267....................$80.00–90.00
Plate 268....................$45.00–55.00
Plate 269....................$65.00–75.00
Plate 270....................$75.00–85.00
Plate 271..................$175.00–200.00
Plate 272.....................(see Plate 271)
Plate 273. ....set $80.00–100.00
Plate 274. ....set $225.00–250.00
Plate 275..................$150.00–175.00
Plate 276....................$45.00–55.00
Plate 277..................$225.00–250.00
Plate 278..................$350.00–400.00
Plate 279..................$250.00–300.00
Plate 280....................$65.00–75.00
Plate 281....................$30.00–40.00
Plate 282..................$125.00–150.00
Plate 283..................$100.00–120.00
Plate 284..................$125.00–150.00
Plate 285. ....ea. $125.00–150.00
Plate 286. ....ea. $400.00–500.00
Plate 287..................$200.00–225.00
Plate 288..................$250.00–300.00
Plate 289..................$200.00–225.00

Plate 290....................$45.00–55.00
Plate 291..................$140.00–160.00
Plate 292..................$160.00–185.00
Plate 293....................$60.00–80.00
Plate 294....................$35.00–45.00
Plate 295....................$65.00–75.00
Plate 296....................$80.00–100.00
Plate 297..................$225.00–250.00
Plate 298..................$100.00–125.00
Plate 299..................$125.00–150.00
Plate 300....................$75.00–90.00
Plate 301..................$275.00–325.00
Plate 302..................$150.00–175.00
Plate 303..................$125.00–150.00
Plate 304. ....ea. $125.00–150.00
Plate 305 Dinner Plate...$25.00–35.00
          Salad Plate $20.00–25.00
          Bread & Butter Plate..$14.00–18.00
          Cup & Saucer...........$25.00–30.00
          Fruit Bowl $15.00–20.00
Plate 306. Dinner Plate..$25.00–35.00
          Luncheon Plate $20.00–30.00
          Salad Plate $15.00–25.00
          Soup Bowl $25.00–35.00
          Bread & Butter Plate..$15.00–18.00
          Butter Pat $20.00–25.00
          Cup & Saucer...........$25.00–30.00
          Fruit Bowl $14.00–18.00
Plate 307. Dinner Plate..$20.00–30.00
          Salad Plate $15.00–20.00
          Soup/Cereal Bowl $15.00–20.00
          Cup & Saucer...........$20.00–30.00
Plate 308. Dinner Plate..$15.00–20.00
          Bread & Butter Plate ..$8.00–12.00
          Fruit Bowl $8.00–12.00
          Cup & Saucer...........$15.00–20.00
Plate 309....................$55.00–65.00
Plate 310....................$55.00–65.00
Plate 311....................$10.00–15.00
Plate 312....................$70.00–80.00
Plate 313....................$60.00–70.00
Plate 314..................$250.00–275.00
Plate 315..................$275.00–300.00
Plate 316....................$75.00–100.00
Plate 317..................$250.00–300.00
Plate 318....................$75.00–100.00
Plate 319..................$350.00–375.00
Plate 320..................$100.00–120.00
Plate 321....................$30.00–40.00
Plate 322....................$60.00–75.00
Plate 323....................$50.00–60.00
Plate 324....................$90.00–110.00
Plate 325.....................(see Plate 324)
Plate 326....................$75.00–85.00
Plate 327.....................(see Plate 326)
Plate 328....................$70.00–80.00
Plate 329....................$15.00–18.00
Plate 330....................$50.00–60.00
Plate 331....................$20.00–30.00
Plate 332....................$30.00–35.00
Plate 333....................$45.00–55.00
Plate 334. Left $18.00–22.00
          Right $25.00–30.00
Plate 335....................$80.00–100.00

Plate 336.................$100.00–120.00
Plate 337.................$15.00–20.00
Plate 338.................$50.00–60.00
Plate 339.................$75.00–85.00
Plate 340.................$45.00–55.00
Plate 341.................$45.00–55.00
Plate 342.................$65.00–75.00
Plate 343.................$30.00–40.00
Plate 344.................$35.00–45.00
Plate 345.................$150.00–175.00
Plate 346.................$150.00–175.00
Plate 347.................$75.00–85.00
Plate 348.................$55.00–65.00
Plate 349.................$70.00–80.00
Plate 350.................$20.00–25.00
Plate 351.................$10.00–15.00
Plate 352.................$10.00–15.00
Plate 353.................$15.00–20.00
Plate 354.................$14.00–18.00
Plate 355.................$75.00–85.00
Plate 356.................$85.00–95.00
Plate 357.................$55.00–65.00
Plate 358.................$8.00–12.00
Plate 359.................$25.00–30.00
Plate 360.................$20.00–25.00
Plate 361.................$25.00–30.00
Plate 362.................$20.00–25.00
Plate 363.................$20.00–25.00
Plate 364.................$20.00–25.00
Plate 365.................$15.00–20.00
Plate 366.................$250.00–300.00
Plate 367.................$275.00–325.00
Plate 368. ....set $30.00–40.00
Plate 369.................$45.00–55.00
Plate 370.................$50.00–60.00
Plate 371.................$20.00–25.00
Plate 372.................$20.00–25.00
Plate 373.................$45.00–55.00
Plate 374.................$55.00–65.00
Plate 375.................$240.00–260.00
Plate 376.................$45.00–55.00
Plate 377.................$100.00–120.00
Plate 378. ....$75.00–100.00
Plate 379.................$35.00–45.00
Plate 380.................$225.00–250.00
Plate 381.................$150.00–175.00
Plate 382. ....(mc) $80.00–100.00
Plate 383.................$35.00–45.00
Plate 384.................$50.00–60.00
Plate 385.................$80.00–90.00
Plate 386.................$60.00–70.00
Plate 387.................$275.00–300.00
Plate 388.................$140.00–160.00
Plate 389.................$275.00–325.00
Plate 390.................$325.00–375.00
Plate 391.................$120.00–140.00
Plate 392.................$75.00–85.00
Plate 393.................$60.00–70.00
Plate 394.................$75.00–85.00
Plate 395. ....$40.00–50.00
Plate 396.................$25.00–30.00
Plate 397.................$55.00–65.00
Plate 398. ....set $250.00–300.00
Plate 399.................$80.00–100.00

Plate 400. ....ea. $120.00–135.00
Plate 401.................$100.00–125.00
Plate 402.................$175.00–200.00
Plate 403.................$10.00–15.00
Plate 404.............pair $40.00–50.00
Plate 405. Left........pr. $30.00–40.00
        Others ...pr. $20.00–30.00
Plate 406. ....pr. $15.00–20.00
Plate 407. ....pr. $20.00–25.00
Plate 408.................$275.00–300.00
Plate 409.................$80.00–100.00
Plate 410.................$35.00–40.00
Plate 411.................$45.00–50.00
Plate 412.................$50.00–60.00
Plate 413.................$45.00–55.00
Plate 414. ....set $150.00–175.00
Plate 415.................$60.00–75.00
Plate 416.................$75.00–85.00
Plate 417. ...complete $120.00–140.00
Plate 418.................$40.00–50.00
Plate 419.................$150.00–160.00
Plate 420.................$45.00–55.00
Plate 421.................$20.00–25.00
Plate 422.................$25.00–35.00
Plate 423.................$600.00–700.00
Plate 424.................$700.00–800.00
Plate 425. w/o lid $120.00–140.00
Plate 426. w/o lid $120.00–140.00
Plate 427. w/o lid $120.00–140.00
Plate 428.................$220.00–240.00
Plate 429.................$250.00–275.00
Plate 430.................$120.00–135.00
Plate 431. ....ea. $30.00–35.00
Plate 432. Left $225.00–275.00
        Right $275.00–325.00
Plate 433.................$120.00–140.00
Plate 434.................$120.00–140.00
Plate 435. Teapot.....$225.00–250.00
        Trivet......$120.00–140.00
Plate 436.................$150.00–175.00
Plate 437.................$150.00–175.00
Plate 438. Teapot.....$200.00–225.00
     Sugar & Creamer..$125.00–150.00
Plate 439.................$250.00–275.00
Plate 440.................$120.00–140.00
Plate 441.................$225.00–250.00
Plate 442.................$225.00–250.00
Plate 443.................$175.00–200.00
Plate 444.................$50.00–65.00
Plate 445. Left $150.00–175.00
        Right $80.00–100.00
Plate 446.................$60.00–75.00
Plate 447.................$50.00–60.00
Plate 448.................$35.00–45.00
Plate 449.................$100.00–120.00
Plate 450.................$120.00–140.00
Plate 451.................$80.00–100.00
Plate 452. Teapot.........$50.00–60.00
     Cup & Saucer.........$25.00–35.00
Plate 453. Teapot.....$200.00–225.00
        Trivet $75.00–100.00
Plate 454. Teapot.....$275.00–300.00
     Creamer & Sugar...$250.00–300.00
     Lg. Cup & Saucer $80.00–100.00

Sm. Cup & Saucer.....$60.00–80.00
Plate 455.................$175.00–200.00
Plate 456.................$70.00–80.00
Plate 457.................$75.00–85.00
Plate 458.................$90.00–100.00
Plate 459.................$55.00–65.00
Plate 460.................$125.00–150.00
Plate 461.................$80.00–90.00
Plate 462.................$130.00–145.00
Plate 463. ....$1,400.00–1,600.00
Plate 464.................$80.00–100.00
Plate 465..........ea. $800.00–1,000.00
Plate 466.................$45.00–55.00
Plate 467.................$50.00–60.00
Plate 468.................$35.00–45.00
Plate 469.................$125.00–150.00
Plate 470.................$120.00–135.00
Plate 471.................$125.00–150.00
Plate 472.................$35.00–45.00
Plate 473.................$80.00–90.00
Plate 474..........pair $300.00–350.00
Plate 475..........pair $250.00–300.00
Plate 476.................$300.00–350.00
Plate 477.................$300.00–350.00
Plate 478.................$300.00–350.00
Plate 479.................$400.00–500.00
Plate 480.................$600.00–700.00
Plate 481.................$400.00–450.00
Plate 482.................$120.00–140.00
Plate 483.................$55.00–65.00
Plate 484.................$40.00–50.00
Plate 485........set $1,400.00–1,600.00
Plate 486.................$225.00–250.00
Plate 487.................$150.00–175.00
Plate 488.................$325.00–375.00
Plate 489.......set $1,200.00–1,400.00
Plate 490..........set $800.00–1,000.00
Plate 491........set $1,400.00–1,600.00
Plate 492.................$300.00–350.00
Plate 493.......set $1,000.00–1,200.00
Plate 494.................$375.00–425.00
Plate 495.................set $57.00
Plate 496.................$30.00
Plate 497. Salt & Pepper set.....$18.00
     Gravy w/underplate $27.00
Plate 498.................pair $42.50
Plate 499. ....$20.00
Plate 500.................set $69.00
Plate 501.................$20.00
Plate 502.................$35.00
Plate 503.................$50.00
Plate 504.................set $15.00
Plate 505..................ea. $15.00
Plate 506..................set $50.00
Plate 507. ....$30.00

*Note that prices for Plates 495 through 507
are retail catalog prices for 1985–1987 for pro-
duction in those years (see page 173). Prices
are not quoted for Plates 508 through 520 due
to the nature of the items which serve as
examples of how the Willow pattern has been
used in art work, advertising, and paper and
plastic products.